Information
need

Information need

A Theory Connecting Information Search to Knowledge Formation

Charles Cole

ASIST Monograph Series

Published on behalf of the
American Society for Information Science and Technology by

Information Today, Inc.
Medford, New Jersey

First printing, 2012

Information Need: A Theory Connecting Information Search to
Knowledge Formation

Library of Congress Cataloging-in-Publication Data

Cole, Charles, 1953-
 Information need : a theory connecting information search to knowledge
formation / by Charles Cole.
       p. cm. -- (ASIS&T monograph series)
   Includes bibliographical references and index.
   ISBN 978-1-57387-429-8
      1. Information behavior. 2. Information retrieval. 3. Information storage and retrieval
systems. 4. Human information processing. 5. Knowledge, Theory of. 6. Information
theory I. Title.
   ZA3075.C64 2012
   025.5'24--dc23

                                                                            2011051294

President and CEO: Thomas H. Hogan, Sr.
Editor-in-Chief and Publisher: John B. Bryans
VP Graphics and Production: M. Heide Dengler
Managing Editor: Amy M. Reeve
ASIST Monograph Series Editor: Samantha Hastings
Editorial Assistant: Brandi Scardilli
Book Designer: Kara Mia Jalkowski
Cover Designer: Denise Erickson
Copyeditor: Dorothy Pike
Proofreader: Penelope Mathiesen
Indexer: Becky Hornyak

Contents

PART III: APPLICATION OF THE THEORY OF INFORMATION NEED TO INFORMATION SYSTEM DESIGN

PART IV: CONCLUSION

Introduction

Information need is not a traditional need like the need for food, water, shelter. In those needs, the human organism knows at once there is a need and what is required to satisfy the need. Contrary to this, information need occurs at the oddest time; you don't know you need a particular piece of information, so you don't conduct a search for information you don't need; then, when you find it, you realize you need it. Information need seems to work in reverse order—at least in some cases. In other cases you know the information already but you need to hear it again, or from a certain source or channel of communication. Some channels are hot, some cool. You have an exploratory information need and a confirmation need.

Let us give an example of a cut-and-dry information need situation. A teenage boy and girl are walking down the street towards a movie theatre. They are not together, just friends since childhood. They talk about text messaging their friends because they need the exact start time for the movie, but then they remember their smartphone can give them this information via the internet. "We don't have to bother them," the girl says. "But it is more interesting to text message," the boy says. He adds, "Actually, I think I'll phone them. I can ask about their colds. The two of them were sniffing yesterday. Where did they say they'd be? Are they driving?" "Pleeeease," the girl says. "Give me that." She grabs the phone from the boy's hand and quickly web searches for the movie website to obtain the start time. "There: Nine-fifteen. It is really just confirmation," she explains. "No use interrupting them. Why don't we go in here for a coffee; we have time." The boy says nothing. He walks on, then notices his friend is entering a coffee shop but is reluctant to follow. She turns and looks straight at him. "Are you coming?" she asks. He follows her inside. Different information needs, different channels of seeking the information; there are exploratory information needs and confirmation information needs. But information need is more complex than this.

The author can recall an information need incident that occurred in January 2011 while he was watching an interview on CNN about the link between autism and childhood vaccinations. This decades-old story had recently taken a new twist, bringing it into the news again ("Study linking vaccine to autism is called fraud," *New York*

Times, January 6, 2011, p. A10). The story began in 1998 with the appearance of a study by Dr. Wakefield, et al., in the legendary journal *The Lancet*. Discrepancies in Dr. Wakefield's methodology were discovered soon after. Ten of Wakefield's co-authors renounced the study, causing *The Lancet* to withdraw the article. Recently, and this is where the CNN interview comes in, independent researchers re-examined the data from the 12 subjects in the 1998 study and found that Dr. Wakefield and his colleagues had altered facts about the 12 subjects in the original 1998 study, alterations which amounted to fraud. Well-known CNN commentator Dr. Sanjay Gupta was calmly explaining why Dr. Wakefield's study, which buttressed the anti-vaccination argument, had been so dangerous to society as a whole. Dr. Gupta was discussing the vaccination story at a high level and in a serious manner using medical terminology that this author finds increasingly interesting as he gets older.

Dr. Gupta suddenly used the term "herd immunity." He said that the nonvaccinated children threatened those children who were immunized due to "herd immunity." Not to misquote Dr. Gupta, the author went back the next day to the CNN website to retrieve the archived transcript from the Parker-Spitzer show (transcripts.cnn.com/TRANSCRIPTS/1101/05/ps.01.html):

> At one point the vaccination rates dropped below 80 percent. Now what vaccinations sort of count on is what's known as a herd immunity. You're vaccinated, therefore, I'm more protected. Kathleen [Parker, the show's co-animator] is more protected. If we're all vaccinated, we protect everyone in the room. If one person drops out, then all of a sudden you start to put all of those people at risk. If you look at the numbers, they say, unless you get above 95 percent vaccination, herd immunity sort of falls apart.

The Dr. Gupta segment ended. Several minutes later, an epidemiologist walked into the room where the author was sitting. The author asked the epidemiologist about the term "herd immunity." The epidemiologist answered that herd immunity was a 95 percent threshold. Because the anti-vaccination movement stimulated by Dr. Wakefield's 1998 publication had prevented the herd immunity threshold from being met, nonvaccinated children who were carriers of the disease now threatened other nonvaccinated children if they by chance came into contact with them. This possibility would occur more frequently if vaccination rates dropped below 95 percent. The epidemiologist said there were several geographical pockets in the U.S. where vaccination rates had dropped to the 80 percent mark, leading to an outbreak in measles.

For some reason the author felt uneasiness, but the feeling did not register at the conscious level right away. Then he became aware of the feeling of unease but he could not relate the uneasiness to anything in particular at that moment. In retrospect, he realized that the sense of unease occurred because of something the epidemiologist had said. The epidemiologist said that nonvaccinated children threatened other nonvaccinated children. In retrospect, the author realized he had had the contrary impression when listening to Dr. Gupta—that Gupta was referring to the transference of the disease from nonvaccinated to *vaccinated children.*

Unprompted, the epidemiologist then added a key phrase to his explanation of the "herd immunity." He said that the herd immunity also pertained to the fact that in some children the vaccination against measles does not take, giving it no effect, thus rendering these children vulnerable to the disease if they happened to come into contact with it. This subgroup of vaccinated children is vulnerable to catching the disease if the vaccination rate goes below 95 percent of the population, and it is this group Dr. Gupta was talking about.

Only when the epidemiologist, quite by accident, satisfied the author's information need, did the author realize he had had an information need.

Let us analyze the information need of the author, who will be referred to as "the information user":

1. The information need centering on the term "herd immunity" first occurred, which the user was not aware of either affectively or cognitively.

2. A minute or two later, the user became affectively aware of an information need when he noticed his feeling of unease. He felt at a visceral level that what the epidemiologist said about the transmission route disagreed with the user's impression of Dr. Gupta's discussion of the transmission route. At this point, the user could not relate the feeling of unease to any particular notion, problem, or issue.

3. The user then engaged in nonpurposive information behavior by talking to the epidemiologist about the term "herd immunity."

4. The epidemiologist said that immunization does not take effect in some children, leaving them vulnerable to infection if the vaccination rate in the general population falls below the 95 percent level.

5. The user became cognitively aware of his information need when he received the information from the epidemiologist that satisfied the information need.

6. The information user was also aware that his belief system and/or knowledge system was involved, "flowing in" (if that's the right term). The information about herd immunity seemed to coincide with the author's belief that the world works in probabilities rather than a yes/no perspective and that statements in science and medicine in particular must leave room for other possible explanations for a given event. Perhaps this is how our minds work best!

This book offers a new perspective on information need that takes this need as being anchored in the neurology of the brain. How do we naturally think through problems, make reasonable decisions—and unreasonable decisions? And how do we make use of information to perform a task? If we could get at why the human perceptual and cognitive systems seek out information, why these systems almost force us to look for information, or to recognize our need for information suddenly when we are thinking of something else, and if we could get at how these systems work to make use of needed information—i.e., how information need works—couldn't we then build this knowledge into more natural thinking information systems?

The perspective takes advantage of the recent advancement in evolutionary psychology, which seeks to find out, for example, why and how modern humans survived while our Neanderthal cousins did not. This field is trying to get at, among other things, why and how modern humans needed, sought, and used information that was different from the Neanderthals. Could we then utilize these fundamental aspects of information need, why and how it works, to build into intuitive working information systems?

The mobility and ease of use of recent information system (retrieval) technology seems to point in the direction of providing information need and use devices at every moment of the day or night, allowing access to an increasing portion of human knowledge at our fingertips. The trade name Google has turned into the verb Googling due to its commonplaceness in our daily lives. Googling means something like: the activity of being enabled by mobile technological devices to look up information at any time we need it—at home, at the office, or even when we are on the move via our cell phones or iPads.

The negative side of this constant need for information, judging from the advertisements for cell phones, apps, and the like, is creating a caricature of human life, turning it into something like a constant Trivial Pursuit game, with everyone, especially young people, continuously and obsessively needing to look up information or "facts" as they walk down the street. These facts include the location of a friend or an event, or the mood a friend is in, for every moment during the day or night.

But it means something different, something more profound. Mobile information system technology assumes—and sales figures seem to prove—that these devices are allowing us to be more natural, more human; that we were prevented before from exercising our human need for information at any time of the day or night by clunky information systems and the division of society into the educated classes and the vast majority who could barely read.

It is early going in our era of ubiquitous information need and use, but there is a paradox developing. Despite the fact that human beings are better educated than ever before, and that we now have the easy and constant ability to exercise our need for information through the internet anywhere and at any time of the day or night on our mobile devices, to look up any information we need, hundreds of millions of people who own technology devices don't use information beyond needing and looking up facts. There seems to be a huge side of information need, through Facebook, Twitter, etc., that is centered on where we are and how we feel about things in relation to other people in our physical and social environment. Some would say this type of need and use of information does not utilize the deeper power, the deeper levels of information, information need, and information use: the knowledge side of the data-information-knowledge continuum.

The last sentence is somewhat controversial. Some say there is no deeper level to information need and use than the need and use of factual information. That knowledge formation should not be the concern of information systems, information accessing, or information retrieval (IR) devices. Knowledge formation, they believe, is the purview of educational technology systems.

Let us simplify the division of opinion on this issue by saying there is a division between the two sciences concerned with information need, why we need information, and how it works; between information science on the one hand and computer science on the other. Information science is a unique science that investigates the human side of information need and use, and makes recommendations to the computer scientists who develop the information systems and mobile information accessing devices. That information science is or should be concerned with knowledge formation has long been pointed out (Kochen, 1969; see also Brittain, 1970). Computer science, however, builds information systems under the assumption that people need and seek fact- or answer-based information. We have structured this book around the debate over information need between information science and computer science.

It is difficult for students and researchers on either side of the debate to understand what the other side means. It is as though the two sides see the same reality but through different eyes, a different perspective. This book sets out to understand the two sides, and to create a theory of information need that is the interplay between the two perspectives. For example, the computer science notion of information need and use that is fact- or answer-seeking-based is incorporated in the information need theory we propose as a first phase to information need and use leading to knowledge formation.

This book proposes a theory of information need that provides the basis for the design of information systems based on engaging the user's knowledge formation systems. The principle is that if information technology and the ability to utilize information are to be available for everyone, and the ability of information systems to act as one with the human brain is to become a reality in the near future, then information search must involve human knowledge formation.

The book is divided into four parts.

Part I investigates the what and why of information need: what it is and why humans need information. The goal of Part I is to carefully analyze Taylor's (1968) influential four-level information need model, which posits the deepest level as intangible and nonspecifiable—"a description of an area of doubt" that is "inexpressible in linguistic terms" (Taylor, 1968, pp. 179, 182). Starting from Taylor's four-level model of information need, we will show a theoretical outline for a knowledge-based rather than the purely information-based theory of information need of present IR system design, a nuance Taylor acknowledged "may" be at the heart of his model (Taylor, 1968, p. 189).

Part II investigates how information need works. Drawing on data collected in a study of 45 history PhD students, Part II illustrates how information need works in two distinct information search situations: 1) When the user of an information system is in a Pre-focus or exploratory information search mode, and 2) When the user of an information system is in a Focusing mode of information search. The data illustrate how information need is created.

Part III gives an example of an information system device that facilitates users instantiating their information need and making it work for them to perform a task. The task illustrated is undergraduate students utilizing an information system to research and write a social science essay.

Part IV offers a short conclusion. The ultimate goal of presenting a theory of information need is to contribute to the design of information or IR systems that will 1) ameliorate the information overload problem associated with system output in the results list of today's IR systems for the majority of users, and 2) facilitate the utilization of information and IR systems, via human information need-oriented design, for a greater cross-section of the population, especially for information-disadvantaged groups in our information age (like "oil-flow," we should be concerned with information flow to disadvantaged populations) (Langlois, 1983, p. 587).

Part **I**

Definition of
Information Need

CHAPTER 1

The Importance of Information Need

Information need is the motivation people think and feel to seek information, but it is a complex concept that divides researchers. In this chapter, we discuss preliminary definitions of information need derived from a historical and current overview of the concept in computer and information science. We set our discussion of information need firmly inside information search. This is a solitary activity between a human and a machine. The information search is conducted via some sort of device or tool, usually a computer, iPad, or, increasingly, a mobile phone or smartphone. Such devices have the capability of being an extension of not only the human mind but also, via the internet, of all of human memory, all of human knowledge.

This book proposes a theory of information need for information retrieval (IR). Information need traditionally denotes the start state for someone seeking information. This involves all sorts of information seeking (purposive information behavior) and the broader still human information behavior (which also includes non-purposive information behavior) (Wilson, 1999). Here we limit our discussion to information search involving user interaction with an information system, which can be a search engine such as Google, an online public access catalog (OPAC), or any of the scholarly or research-oriented retrieval systems such as PsycINFO, Historical Abstracts, or PubMED.

There are two perspectives on information need for information search: a computer science perspective and an information science perspective. Information search system design is dominated by a computer science perspective where the user's information need is to find an answer, the form of which is known by the user beforehand; the query to the information system is not so much a question as a demand to obtain this specific form of answer. The user then takes away the answer, which is the system output. The computer science perspective comes, in its most basic form, from an engineering tradition of humans turning on a machine, getting it to work with an appropriate human command input, then taking away the machine output. In this perspective, it is easy for the user to formulate the demand for answer-based information into a query-command to the system (Nicolaisen, 2009).

The information seeking perspective takes the larger and contrary view, that the user often needs information to fill out a conceptualization of a problem or idea. The user very much wants this information. The user from this perspective doesn't know the answer he/she is searching for and therefore finds it difficult to formulate a query to the system. The query, as a formulation of the user's information need, must in a certain sense open the door to information flow, which is controlled by, in general terms, what the user already knows, thinks, and believes, and the neurological architecture of the reasoning part of the brain. The book attempts to understand and explain these two perspectives and develops a theory of information need that is an interplay between these two perspectives.

In Figure 1.1, we diagram the difference between the computer science (left-hand side of the figure) and the information science (right-hand side) perspective on this fundamental purpose of information need. The computer science perspective conceptualizes the user's information need as the input into the information system or "Web-Component" in the figure, which produces the answer output. Far from being critical of the computer science point of view, in

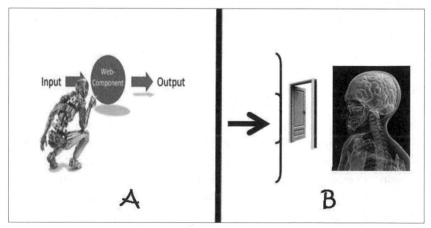

Figure 1.1 Two conceptions of information need: A) computer science "input-output" and B) information science, where information need opens the door to the user's perceptual and cognitive system

Chapter 8 at the end of Part I, we indicate that it describes information need in a post-focus phase of performing a task or solving a problem.

Information science conceptualizes the user's information need as a gap in understanding that opens the door to let in information from the textual environment—an information system, for example. Between the user's (sensory) perceptual and cognitive system and information flow coming at the user via environmental stimuli from the outside world is a four-pronged symbol representing the interface between the user and the environment. We utilize the four-pronged symbol throughout the book to represent this interface. While in Part I we begin by examining this information flow from environment to person in a general sense, the focus of this book is the information flow from the textual environment of an information system—the text and symbols on the computer screen representing the system's information, particularly the results list—to the user's perceptual-cognitive and knowledge processing systems.

CHAPTER 2

The History of
Information Need

The information science perspective on the user and information need is ambiguous and complex. Though perhaps going back as far as the 1940s (Bernal, 1948; Urquhart, 1948), it took form in the 1960s and early 1970s in chapters in the *Annual Review of Information Science and Technology* (*ARIST*) entitled "Information Needs and Uses." These chapters associated the concepts of need and use, either struggling to differentiate the two concepts or treating need and use as the same thing. A needs assessment study, for example, denoted frequency of use or satisfaction with the sources or channels of accessing information made available in the library or information center of a corporation, so that library administrators could make service decisions (Paisley, 1968, p. 21; for an example, see Menzel, 1966). Differentiating the two concepts was difficult "operationally, if not philosophically" (Lipetz, 1970, p. 26). There are three traditions existing today, expressed in the early *ARIST* review chapters, that reveal this uneasy alliance between the concepts of use and need.

The *first tradition* in these early *ARIST* chapters is the treatment of information need as both a psychological and sociological concept (see also Brittain, 1970, p. 10). Influenced by Shannon's (1949) seminal paper on communication (information) flow between a source and a receiver over a communication channel (see further discussion later in the chapter), information science researchers studied information flow over various channels, which became divided into formal and informal channels. Formal channels were defined as tools or systems placed at the user's disposal in libraries or information centers (of corporations). Informal channels were defined as conversations with others. The researchers were struck by the observation of the importance of informal channels of accessing information for the researchers and technologists studied. As these informal channels were contacts with other people, this established an interest in the sociological basis of the variance in information need.

The sociological aspect of information need focused on the term "invisible college"; this was an aspect of need that seemed to occur during the early stages of a project, in the idea-formation stage (Lin and Garvey, 1972). The subjects in the studies hashed out their ideas with colleagues they trusted in the field. The advantages of this informal channel of information flow were its flexibility, the "rapid" almost immediate feedback, for example, the pointing out of implications of a concept or research results by the colleague, etc. (Menzel, 1968; see also Brittain, 1970, pp. 78–80; Lipetz, 1970). Wolek (1970) attempted to understand the greater reliance on interpersonal or informal communication flow by defining its importance to mission-oriented tasks, as compared to basic research by exploring the hypothesis that "the probability that a communication will involve interpersonal interaction between source and receiver varies directly with the complexity of the message communicated" (quoted in Crane, 1971, p. 29).

The sociological aspect took a conceptual turn when Paisley (1968) then Allen (1969) organized their *ARIST* review chapters of needs and uses studies into concentric circles that constitute ever-wider information systems in which the individual researcher seeks information.

Paisley originally diagrammed the channels in 10 concentric circles. The individual researcher's first channel or source of information is the innermost circle: "the scientist within his own head" (Paisley, 1968, p. 6). This declares information need importantly, perhaps fundamentally, as a concept rooted in psychology. The other nine circles, however, were sociological. In Paisley's channel conceptualization, the next concentric circle of the 10, and first outside channel of information seeking, is the researcher's conversations with work team colleagues in the same organization. The broadest circle or system is the researcher within a formal information system such as a library or information center. Paisley defined the innermost circle, the scientist within his own head, as constituting the researcher's motivation, intelligence, creativity, cognitive structure, system of perceived relevance, and system "of information inputs and uses of information outputs" (Paisley, 1968, p. 6). To simplify, we have diagrammed Allen's (1969, pp. 4–5) reduction of Paisley's (1968) 10 concentric circles to six concentric circles in Figure 2.1.

In his *ARIST* review chapter, Allen (1969) incorporated Paisley's (1968) idea of diagramming information flow from various sources

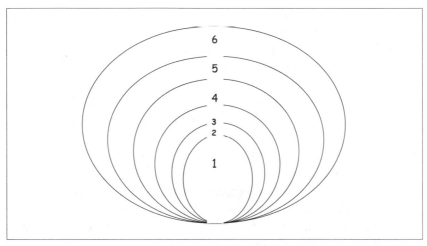

Figure 2.1   Concentric circles representing formal (circle 6) and informal (circles 1–5) channels of information flow in user information search

(channels) to the user in six concentric circles, beginning with the information flows of the user 1) inside his or her own head, which Allen relabeled "the individual as an information processor" (Allen, 1969, p. 5). From this innermost circle, information flow widens to the user's 2) research group, 3) organization, 4) professional society, and 5) invisible college. The largest circle is 6) the user in a formal information system such as a library or information center in a corporation.

In his six concentric circles categorizing channel types, Allen combines the psychological aspect (circle 1 in Figure 2.1) with the sociological aspects of information need; for the sociological aspect he takes into account both informal channels of information flow (circles 2–5) and formal channels (circle 6). In the innermost circle, constituting what is inside the user's head as an information processor, Allen focuses on the user's use of information to effectuate his or her cognitive state. Specifically, information use changes the probabilities in the set of likely solutions to a problem, adds new likely solutions, or deletes them from the set. At a certain point, the probability, which can be associated with an uncertainty measure (see later discussion in the chapter), rises to the point where one member of the set is selected over all the others in the set as the solution to a problem or task. Information use effectuates these changes in probability calculations, and it is possible that a definition of information need has something to do with the need to increase the probability of one member of the set of likely solutions to the point where the user can go forward with the selection.

To explicate this operationalization of the effect of information need on the user's cognitive state, we refer to Allen's (1966) MIT study utilizing critical incident decision methodology. These studies took place inside corporations among the project teams working on 19 separate Research and Development (R and D) engineering projects (Allen, 1966, p. 12). Project leaders kept a Solution Development Record for each real-life problem the engineering team faced. For the Solution Development Record form, the project leader 1) created a set of likely solutions to the current problem, and 2) gave an "initial estimate of the likelihood that each of the possible alternative solutions would eventually be adopted" (Allen, 1966, p. 4; see also Menzel, 1966, p. 65). These likelihood estimates were revised weekly by the project leader, with Allen noting changes in probability estimates for each member of the set of alternative solutions, the information that stimulated the change, and the channel through which the information was accessed. Any new solution alternatives could be added to the set in a blank space at the bottom of the form.

We give a detailed description of the Solution Development Record form for two sample problems taken from Allen (1966). We also diagram visualization of the two problems in Figure 2.2. The data for these Allen studies were collected from real R and D departments for real engineering problems; due to the sensitive nature of the data, Allen gives sample problems that are fictitious (Allen, personal communication, January 13, 2011). Problem 1 concerns a set of three alternative solutions, and at some point during the problem–solution time line, the project team was "completely uncommitted" to either of alternative solutions 1 and 3. The project leader circled 0.5 probability for each on the Solution Development Record for that week, and indicated no probability estimation for alternative 2:

1. Orbital rendezvous mission with excursion vehicle: 0.5 probability

2. Orbital rendezvous mission without excursion vehicle: no probability indicated by project leader

3. Direct mission: 0.5 probability (Allen, 1966, p. 5, Figure 1)

Problem 2 is for a space flight to Uranus project specifically concerned with the "design of the electrical power supply system of the vehicle." At the beginning of the study, five likely alternative solutions

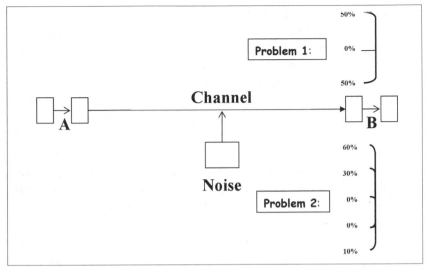

Figure 2.2 Shannon's channel of communication (information) flow between sender (A) and receiver (B) for Allen's problem 1 and problem 2

for this electrical power supply system problem were listed by the project leader, as well as estimated probabilities for each alternative that it would be employed as the final solution to the problem. The project leader was asked to circle on an 11-point scale, from 0 probability to 1.0 probability (certitude). For a sample week, the alternative solutions and their probabilities were:

1. Hydrogen-oxygen fuel cell: 0.6 probability

2. KOH fuel cell: 0.3 probability

3. Ranking cycle fast reactor: no probability indicated by project leader

4. Ranking cycle thermal reactor: no probability indicated by project leader

5. Brayton cycle reactor: 0.1 probability (Allen, 1966, p. 5, Figure 1)

For both problems 1 and 2, according to Allen, "Eventually as the solution progresses, one alternative will attain a 1.0 probability and the others will become zero" (Allen, 1966, p. 4).

Allen's focus in this study was to see what channels scientists versus engineers utilized, and what channels successful project teams utilized compared to less successful teams, by bringing an outside examiner to evaluate project teams' solutions. He found that scientists received almost three times the number of "messages" (i.e., information) from the "literature" channel (books, journals), which is a formal channel, than the engineers (Allen, 1966, p. 12, Table 2). Compared to the engineers in the study, scientists relied more heavily on these formal, outside information channels. Successful engineering teams relied more on internal informal information channels than less successful engineering teams. Allen concludes that "the [engineer] members of industrial and governmental organizations acquire through common experience, and organizational imposition, shared coding schemes which can be quite different from the schemes held by other members of their particular discipline. This is not true of the academic scientists" (Allen, 1966, pp. 25–26). For academic scientists, the "invisible college" is the coding scheme mediator—in other words, an informal external channel to the scientist's academic (university) department.

Based on this observed difference between technologists and scientists, and to enhance technology transfer, Allen recommends an individual serve as a transducer in the flow of information for engineering departments. Information would enter the organization via such individuals, "who are capable of operating within and transforming between two coding schemes [—i.e., the outside coding scheme and the internal coding scheme]" (Allen, 1966, p. 27).

Figure 2.2 utilizes Shannon's famous channel of communication or information flow between a sender and receiver, which underlines Allen's study design. For Shannon's model of the channel of communication flow to signal transmission between a sender and a receiver, the traditional example for a message is a written text that must be converted by an operator at the sender-end of the channel into Morse Code's dots and dashes. The operator is a human form of a transducer. At the receiving end, another operator transduces the dots and dashes of the received signal back into its English message form. In modern technology, a television program is digitally recorded into 1s and 0s and compressed by a transducer into a signal for transmission to receiving towers or to satellite dishes attached to our homes, where the signal is decompressed back into its message form. In Shannon's language, the sender's message must be encoded by a transducer into a signal which is transmitted (over airwaves or electric wires, for example) to the receiver's transducer, which decodes the signal back into its original message form. Noise may affect the signal, causing information to be lost.

If you are in the audience of a concert, listening to a singer, and someone makes a loud noise, you can almost automatically reconstitute the lost words in the message (the words of the song). If you know the song, you fill in the missing words due to the noise; but even if you don't know the words to the particular song, you can fill in the missing words based on the context of the lyrics surrounding the missing information. Word processing software, Google, etc. utilize algorithms that can fill in missing information like wrongly typed-in words, based on context and knowledge of letter and word frequency.

Shannon utilized the 26 letters of the English alphabet as his message set to illustrate his concept of "noise" and how a sent message suffering information loss due to noise affecting the signal during its transmission could be reconstituted at the receiving end's transducer, based on the context of the whole message and known-beforehand frequencies of the various letters of the English alphabet. The letter "e" is the most frequent letter in the English language; and frequency calculations exist in published tables for every letter in the alphabet. In a certain fashion, the receiver's transducer "expects" certain messages based on prior knowledge of frequencies of the members of the message set and the general message context.

In Allen's study and the two problems presented earlier for the manned Uranus landing problem, the receiver of the message is the project leader. He received the message from a sender or source. These different information sources, or communication (information) flow channels, are divided into formal and informal channels (see Figure 2.1). The focus of Allen's study was to discover from which category of channel the project leader received the most messages.

In Figure 2.3, we diagram Allen's study and conclusions, starting with the concept of formal and informal channels of information flow to the project team leader. The project team leader is the receiver of the information messages. The information messages were sent to the receiver over different channels. We utilize the six channel types from Figure 2.1 here on the left-hand side of Figure 2.3.

The interdependence of the psychological and sociological aspects of information need is further evidenced by the research reviewed in the early *ARIST* review chapters. Engelbert (1960) stated that the vague feeling of information need a user may have is the subjective aspect of the need while the objective aspect of the need "arise[s] in the context of the social circumstances in which the user works" (English translation of the German in Brittain, 1970, p. 2, note 3). Menzel (1967, p. 279), on the other hand, defines the unarticulated

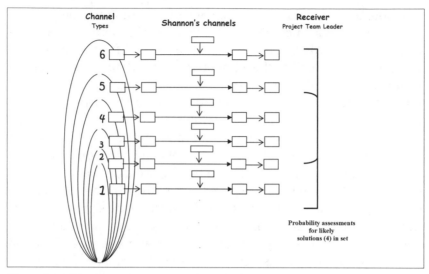

Figure 2.3   Allen's six channel types (concentric circles), Shannon's conceptualization of the information flow channels, and the receiver of the message operationalized as the effect of the received information on the cognitive state of the project leader

need of which the user is unaware into a sociological concept: a need for information that will benefit "the progress of scientific research." The trick is to reconcile the apparent contradictions. Menzel can actually be interpreted to mean that for the user's unarticulated need for information that will benefit the "progress of scientific research," the subject/researcher's first order objective is to make his or her mark in the subject discipline, which can be done via advancing the "progress of scientific research." We refer to this admixture of the psychological and sociological in a full and complex definition of information need in much greater detail later.

But the intriguing part behind the sociological and psychological objectives of the researcher's information need that are served by utilizing informal channels for idea formation is determining how information system design could incorporate the advantages of informal channels, to close the gap between the user's need and the information systems that are designed to satisfy the need (Allen, 1966) by adding "greater flexibility in the formal communication system" via an "increased understanding of the ways in which scientists use ideas and of the types of ideas that are most useful to them" (Crane, 1971, p. 33).

The *second tradition* in these early *ARIST* reviews of research in information need and uses was the attention paid to the subject/researcher's stages of conducting research, and linking the stage to which formal and informal information channels the user selects to utilize when seeking information. The groups studied were often in R and D departments in corporations, with an eye on the efficiency of information flow in these entities. Brittain (1970) in fact complains that there had been, starting in the 1950s, many user studies done of the information behavior of science and technology researchers (both basic research and applied), while there had been very few user studies done of researchers in the social sciences. The researchers utilized different information accessing channels for monitoring a research area, for performing basic research particularly at the "idea" stage, and for applying research by solving problems. The reviews remarked that researchers preferred informal sources or channels of information seeking such as discussions with colleagues in the idea stage, whereas in the problem identification and solving stage they preferred more formal channels.

The researchers in these *ARIST*-reviewed studies who studied researchers and technologists in corporate R and D departments (both basic and applied) "single out the crucial elements of exchange and feedback between an information system and the scientists and technologist (Garvey et al., Paisley, Parker)" (Lin and Garvey, 1972, p. 32). Hence the interest in the advantages of early stage idea formation via utilization of informal channels of information, such as discussions with colleagues. There is this early information science concern for how engineers working in R and D departments in corporations 1) identified a problem, then 2) found ideas for problem solution by accessing information from both library-based or formal channels of information access (Figure 2.4). Harmon (1970) came up with the concept of "cognitive set" to indicate user criteria when seeking information for a project. "Harmon suggests that the cognitive set becomes increasingly sophisticated as inquiry proceeds" (Crane, 1971, p. 23).

The *third tradition* in the early *ARIST* chapters on information needs and uses is that use and need can be treated synonymously, and need and demand can be treated synonymously (Lin and Garvey, 1972, p. 8). Early studies conducted need assessment studies, meaning user "demand" or "use" of various information sources or channels (Brittain, 1970). It is like someone coming up to a counter and demanding or asking the clerk for a book or some known-beforehand

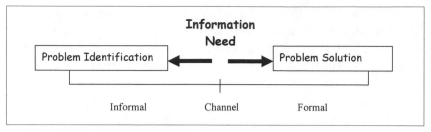

Figure 2.4   Idea formation in problem definition stage versus problem solution stage

item. The clerk is a source or channel of information; the user requests a needed information item from the clerk—"I need such and such a book"—and the clerk satisfies the need by handing the book or item to the user.

When "need" and "demand" are treated synonymously, the assumption is that the user already knows before the search commences the information that is relevant to his work and thus makes a demand on the system for already known information (Brittain, 1970, p. 2). When "need" and "demand" are differentiated, however, "need" is treated by these early information science researchers as a psychological concept (see from this early period, Bernal, 1957; Dannatt, 1967; O'Connor, 1968; Rees, 1963).

In the psychological-based perspective, need becomes an "unarticulated need," where the user "does not have sufficient specific details about the felt need to translate the need into a demand" (Brittain, 1970, p. 2); the unarticulated need is perhaps even unconscious to the user (Menzel, 1967). In such cases, the user only recognizes the information need after the needed information is encountered (Rosenbloom, McLaughlin, and Wolek, 1965; Rosenbloom and Wolek, 1966).The effect of the information, therefore, and the utility of the user utilizing an information system, is to affect the user's cognitive state (Rosenbloom, McLaughlin, and Wolek, 1965; Rosenbloom and Wolek, 1966).

In Figure 2.5, we diagram the association these early *ARIST* chapters made between the three concepts of demand–need–use, based on the users' degree of knowledge about what information they need. In information science, information need is either need-based or demand-based. If we put this on a knowledge continuum or scale, low knowledge about the needed information is correlated with the need as being unarticulated in the user's own mind, while high

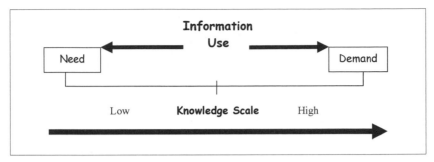

Figure 2.5   Need–demand scale

knowledge about the needed information is correlated with the user making a demand on the information system for the needed and known-about-beforehand information. Figure 2.5 also summarizes the two perspectives on information "use" as outlined in the early *ARIST* chapters: 1) the use of channel to demand and obtain known-about-beforehand information, and 2) in the case of an unarticulated information need, the use of information to affect the user's cognitive state, to increase the "low" knowledge about the information need itself.

This type of perspective on user information need was modeled in 1968 by R. S. Taylor, who favored focusing on the psychological aspect of information need. But he was interested in information system design, and this was the reason for his model of information need. In communicating their information need to an information system—and Taylor was concerned with the pre-electronic era, so he was concerned with the librarian intermediary who in those days frequently intervened between user and the information access systems to actually do the information search—Taylor was interested in the sociological event of a person communicating a deep, psychological need to another person or "information system" (Taylor, 1968, p. 191).

CHAPTER 3

The Framework for
Our Discussion

We first show, through an example of an information need and how it works, the interplay between the information science and computer science perspectives on information need. The information science perspective in this example is a knowledge-formation-based perspective on information need while the computer science perspective is fact- or answer-based. We will then, at the end of this section, operationalize the different perspectives based on Taylor's (1968) influential model of information need.

The framework for this book on information need is the difference between the computer science conception of the user's information need and information science's. The two positions can best be explained via a highly cited model of information need of Taylor (1968) (suggested by Hjørland, 2010). Taylor's model depicted need in four levels:

- Q1: the actual, visceral need, perhaps unconscious to the user

- Q2: the conscious, within-brain description of the need

- Q3: the formalized need; a rational statement of the need

- Q4: the compromised need in language/syntax the user believes is required by the information system (Taylor, 1968, p. 182)

Information science interprets the model vertically, indicating cach information need of every user includes the four levels: a pre-conscious Q1 level underpinning, a conscious inter-brain Q2 level, a formal expression at the Q3 level, as well as a Q4 compromised need level. Computer science, on the other hand, interprets the four-level model horizontally, indicating a phase approach. According to this horizontal or phase perspective, the user comes to the information system only when he or she is in the Q3 phase of the need; at that time, the user fully understands the need and can make a rational statement about it, even formulating the need into a query to the system, which is the compromised Q4 statement of the need. The user may be uncertain about how to formulate the most effective Q4 compromised statement of the need to the information system, but feedback from the results list about the precise terms to use in the query will eliminate the uncertainty. We emphasize the point that in the computer science perspective, the user's original initiating information need is not changed during the search session; only the search terms may be changed in a revised query so that they better conform to the user's originating information need as a result of feedback from the system in the results list (Jansen and Rieh, 2010). MacKay (1969) and Taylor (1968) explain this difference in terms of making a command to the information system (computer science) and asking a question (information science). A command from the user wishes to affect the "goal-setting" levers in the information system, while a question from the user wishes the system to affect the goal-settings, the range of state of readiness, in the user (MacKay, 1969, p. 101). The two distinct interpretations of Taylor's model are illustrated in Figure 3.1.

Information science's vertical interpretation of information need is much more complex and emanates from a fundamentally wider perspective on the user. It is rooted in an information seeking rather than an information search perspective, which predates the development

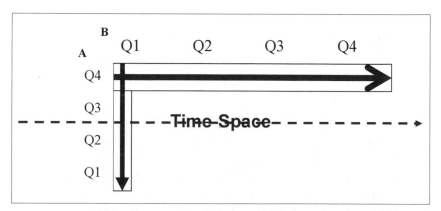

**Figure 3.1   Vertical (A) and horizontal (B) concepts of Taylor's information
         need model**

of widespread electronic information systems. This perspective is a branch of information science research commonly labeled with some variance of the label: "Information Needs, Seeking and Uses." The early summations of such research in the *Annual Review of Information Science and Technology* were given their own chapters entitled: "Information Needs and Uses" (Menzel, 1966; Herner and Herner, 1967; Paisley, 1968; Allen, 1969; Lipetz, 1970; Crane, 1971; Lin and Garvey, 1972; Dervin and Nilan, 1986).

CHAPTER 4

Modeling the User
in Information Search

The traditional model of the user in information search is the user coming to an information system, entering a query, and expecting some sort of specific answer-form from the information system. The key point here is the user's expectation of the answer or answer-form "message" that will be received from the information system.

The traditional model of the user during information search is derived from Shannon's (1949) seminal theory of communication, or theory of information, as it is commonly called (but never by Shannon himself [MacKay, 1953/1955]). In his book, Shannon discusses information in the context of the information situation of a message being sent from the message sender at Point A to a receiver of the message signal at Point B. We should think of an army field situation as Point A where the field officer goes to the communication officer to convert the message in the English language into Morse Code to army command at Point B. The army command's communication officer receives the signal in Morse Code, converts it back to the English language message, and delivers it to army command.

The problem Shannon attacks is the "noise" that enters the message during its signal transmission, which includes errors made by the person at the sender end converting the message into signal form and information dropping out of the signal during transmission. Shannon's theory of communication was designed to measure the information content of the message so that it could be algorithmically corrected at the receiver end. The algorithm can do this because the members of the message set are pre-known by both sender and receiver as are the probabilities (Shannon utilizes as an example the 26 letters of the English alphabet as the message set, whose probabilities, by frequency, are preknown). In a way, this is a very mechanistic or objective modeling of the flow of information from Point A to Point B.

It has been argued that Shannon's theory of information has little or nothing to say about the meaning of a message, and thus that information theory has little to say about a theory of information for information science. The problem, according to MacKay (1983), is that the probabilities in the objective information theory are well-defined and known; for a human subject receiving information messages from the environment, however, we cannot have a well-defined set nor can we know beforehand their respective probabilities. Information science is traditionally concerned by the effect of receiving information on users, particularly how the receivers use the information for a school or work task, or just to make their way through everyday life. This is the difference between the objective perspective on information flow from Point A to Point B and the subjective nature of information flow, which is the concern of information science. The link between the objective description of information flow and psychology, the social sciences, and information science is mainly the work of Donald MacKay (Buckley, 1983, p. 602), whose writings we refer to frequently in this chapter.

However, the underlying conceptual framework of Shannon's theory—the concepts and the interrelationship of these concepts—are well suited to describing the vagaries of how human beings interact with information from the environment, specifically the messages a user receives from an information system. These are: 1) The concept of information in Shannon indicates a subjective reality because it is concerned with "unexpectedness" of the message on the receiver (MacKay, 1983, p. 485), which is appropriate for an information science concept of information; 2) Shannon's concept of the set of likely messages, rather than focusing on just one, operationalizes the "complexity" of the information situation (MacKay, 1983, p. 487; see also Miller, 1983a, p. 493), which is appropriate for an information science concept of information as we describe it later; 3) Shannon's concept of information, with its consideration of the set of all likely possible messages in a given information situation, defines complexity by the "number of alternative forms that [the information situation] might have assumed but did not" (MacKay, 1983, p. 490); 4) Shannon's concept is concerned with the receiver of the message and its "state of conditional readiness" for all possible action (MacKay, 1983, p. 491; we will refer to state of conditional readiness in greater detail later); 5) Shannon's concept considers the response of the message receiver, thus the concern with the receiver's "selection operation on the state of readiness" of the receiver (considered as a "system") (Langlois,

1983, p. 593); 6) Shannon's concept is concerned with relating the magnitude of the information content with the receiver's operation of readiness, as defined by the set of all likely messages, and the selecting operation from the set to establish the "selective information content" (Langlois, 1983, p. 593); 7) And finally, Shannon's concept of information is based on the counter-intuitive notion that "the less probable a message is, the more information it contains" (Miller, 1983a, p. 495). Or the information content of a proposition varies inversely with its probability measure (Carnap, 1950). This is because Shannon is concerned with information "rearrang[ing] the structure of his or her expectations, to alter his or her states of readiness" (Langlois, 1983, p. 598). Shannon's concept of information is counter-intuitive according to a semantic notion of what information is, which positions information as receiving "a lot of data." Shannon, however, is concerned with the information content of the whole information situation. Miller terms this concern as a "measure of selective information, since it has to do with selecting a transmitted message out of the set of all other messages that might have been transmitted instead" (Miller, 1983a, p. 495). Again, we will refer to this in greater detail later.

In Figure 4.1, we illustrate Shannon's classic model of information flow from the sender of a message to the intended receiver. In this model, the sender of the message at Point A sends a message in signal form along a channel to the receiver of the message at Point B. The expected message set, made up of all possible (likely) alternative messages, is indicated by a vertical four-pronged symbol above Point B. The original urgency in Shannon is compensating for information loss during transmission of the signal between Point A and Point B; noise interferes with the transmission, causing information to be lost from the signal and distorting the message received by the receiver. To compensate for information loss, the expected information content of the flow had to be calculated so that redundancy could be built into the signal, which led to Shannon's famous equation of the information content of a message.

We have created a particular information situation in Figure 4.1. The receiver can expect to receive all four likely messages in the set equally as they are, in calculations made before the message was sent, equally probable. As all possible messages that could be sent and received are equi-probable, the information situation and the information content of the message has the highest possible uncertainty. A possible reason for such a situation is that the individual has

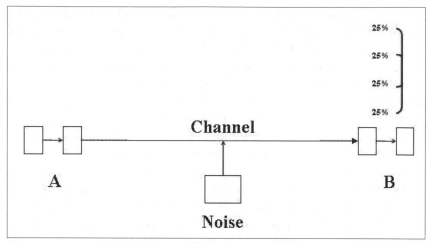

Figure 4.1 Shannon's model of communication or information flow from the
sender, Point A, to the receiver, Point B, which is affected by noise
intrusion distorting the signal and contains an equi-probable set of
expectations indicating a high information content situation

had no previous experience with the phenomenon in the particular
environment. It seems intuitively odd that high information content
of a message is associated with high uncertainty, leading to high
affective uncertainty, information anxiety, and user procrastination
and the avoidance of continuing on with the information search.

Information is difficult (pain-pleasure), a characteristic of information need to which we will return in later discussion. Think about
the highest information content message you have ever received.
Such messages concern life and death issues. A relative is hanging
between life and death. The doctor comes toward you. In your mind,
the probabilities of life or death are equal. In this situation, we prac-
tically faint when we are given the information, it is so powerful. In
Figure 4.1, we expand the message set from two at 50 percent each,
which is the usual high information content situation we face in life,
to a more generic four at 25 percent each. (The four-message set of
equi-probable messages is more generic given the information
search topic of this book.) We maintain this four-message set
throughout the book, codifying it in the four-pronged symbol which
we use over and over again.

The lowest information content situation is where one of the likely
messages in the set is 90 percent to 100 percent likely, relative to the
other members in the set, and this high-likelihood probability is the

one selected by the receiver of the message. Where one member of the set is 100 percent likely, there is zero uncertainty about which signal will be selected by the receiver. In Figure 4.2, we have diagrammed this low uncertainty, low information content situation. Bruner describes this low information situation where one member of the set, which he calls a "hypothesis," has a high expectation likelihood as: "The greater the strength of a hypothesis [versus other possibilities], the less the amount of appropriate information necessary to *confirm it*" (Bruner, 1951, p. 126). Bruner goes on:

> The more frequently a hypothesis or expectancy has been confirmed in the past, the greater will be its strength. Such a frequently confirmed hypothesis will be more readily arousable, will require less environmental information to *confirm it*, and will, conversely, require more contradictory evidence to infirm it [disprove it] than would be required for a less frequently confirmed hypothesis. (Bruner, 1951, p. 126, emphasis added)

Remember that the likelihood probabilities are calculated based on past experience. When clues in the environment cause instantiation of a frame of reference stored in memory, the slots are set to defaults based on past experience. A room frame, for example, has slots indicating walls, a floor, and a roof. These different frame slots

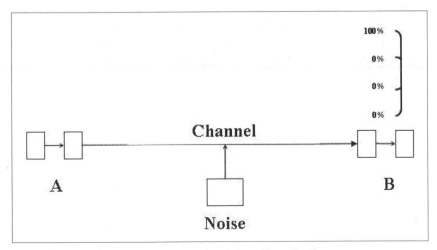

Figure 4.2   Traditional model of user: low information situation

for walls, floor, and roof would be set at close to 100 percent likely, but other alternatives, in a comparative sense, are unlikely but still possible. For example, in a hurricane situation, the roof of the room in the back of a house can be blown off, leaving the front of the house intact. A hurricane situation for an individual who has never seen one, and lives in an area of the world where they never occur, however, is a high information content situation (although it is not for those people who live where hurricanes are common). They go through the front of the house where there is a roof, then at the back of the house they open a door expecting a normal room, and the roof is blown off by the hurricane. What are they thinking at that moment? The point is they are doing a lot of thinking, and they may, in the years that follow, develop a religious principle to explain this act of nature.

Figures 4.1 and 4.2 contrast, respectively, information science's perspective on the user's state of mind when in an exploratory stage of performing a task or project and computer science's traditional model of the user's state of mind. Chapter 5 will illustrate the difference between these two perspectives on the same user's information need.

Computer science models the user with Figure 4.2, a low information content message situation where the user expects a certain answer from the information system, while information science models the user with Figure 4.1, in an exploratory information search, which is a high information content message situation. According to MacKay (1969), information science's perspective of information need is that "It is not a command, as in conventional search strategy, but rather a description of an area of doubt in which the question is open ended, negotiable and dynamic" (Hillman, 1968, quoted in Berul, 1969, p. 210).These are completely different starting premises for the user during information search.

CHAPTER 5

Information Seeking's Conceptualization of Information Need During Information Search

Information science's information seeking perspective on the user's need during information search has several notable features. It has long been interested in dividing information seeking for a user's project or task (a research project, writing an undergraduate essay, finding information for a high school project) into phases, usually with an exploratory first phase followed by phases where the user's information need becomes more specific, as in Rees and Schultz (1967). But in this information seeking perspective, the user seeks information throughout the information need phases, even in the early phases when the user's information need is in an almost unconscious state— i.e., where the user has only a vague notion of a gap or area of not knowing or not understanding something. In fact, the early studies in information seeking research focused on idea generation and problem definition in the R and D departments of technology corporations, and they were specifically interested in the channel or source of the information that led to idea generation and problem definition (e.g., Frischmuth and Allen, 1968).

A second feature of the information seeking perspective is its interest in information seeking beyond the usual so-called formal channels or sources of information to information that is obtained via "informal channels," such as via discussions with colleagues. Baker, Siegmann, and Rubenstein (1967) found that in the early stage of a project, for idea generation and problem definition, informal channels of information seeking were utilized, such as discussions with colleagues inside and outside the company. High employee performance was found to be related to informal channel information seeking (Allen, Gerstenfeld, and Gerstberger, 1968), where "integration" of the information can occur in these personal exchanges (Parker, Lingwood, and Paisley, 1968). Allen (1969) concluded from this finding of the importance of informal channel information seeking where integration of the information can more easily occur that:

> This is not an isolated finding (cf. Baker, Siegmann, and Rubenstein, 1967), but is one to which far too little attention has been paid. It contains an important message for those investigators and research-sponsoring agencies that have focused their attention much too heavily on improving the operation of impersonal [i.e., "formal"] channels. (Allen, 1969, p. 20)

As a result of this wider information seeking perspective on information search, particularly its concern for early stage idea formation and problem definition that have been shown in studies to be best dealt with via informal interpersonal channels, information science has always expressed its criticism of the traditional, computer-science-derived information search model of the user. Information science criticizes the assumption that the user is able to effectively label the information need in the query, believing that it is a much more complicated process than computer science allows for in its model of the user.

5.1 Context of the Information Search: The Problem[atic] Situation

Due to information science's concern for early phase information need during information search, and how to accommodate the flexibility—under determinedness, if you will—of informal channels in the design of formal channel delivery systems (i.e., information system design), the information science perspective assumes that information need starts from a gap in our understanding that is unknowable to the user and nonspecifiable by the user to an information system (Taylor, 1968; for discussion, see Belkin and Vickery, 1985). Users make do by utilizing a compromised form of their real information need in the query to an information system. We will discuss this unknowability/nonspecifiability of information need in great detail throughout the book. It determines the structure and content of the book. For now, we will call it an assumption about information need by information science.

As a result of this assumption, information science's conceptualization of information need in recent decades (since Wilson, 1981) has tended to rest on the assumption that information need is determined by the problem or problematic situation of the user (cf., Belkin and Vickery, 1985). Thus the early information science concern for information flow within a corporation, discussed previously, specifically the informal channels of information flow that involve talking over problems with colleagues both inside and outside the corporation.

There are at least two phases of a problem: 1) identifying or defining the problem and 2) finding a solution to the problem. When we say defining a problem, information science means it in a technical way. This is similar to when an astronaut in space says "Houston, we have a problem." The immediate first step is to define the problem in all its aspects or critical dimensions. The dimensions operationally define the problem. But the added feature of dividing a problem into its dimensions is that "It is also possible to modify the set of dimensions, thus changing the [definition of the] problem" (Allen and Frischmuth, 1968, p. 19).

The problem situation is a sociological construct. It assumes that information need starts from and is determined by the situation in which the user finds the problem. Consequently, according to the information science perspective, it is essential to study and define information need in its sociological context. The added complexity of contextualizing information need as an input into the service of problem identification and solution, or thinking about information need as being conceptually submerged inside a problematic situation, is that all problems are identified and solved in the context of some sociological entity such as an organization, a company, or even a school or university.

The sociological perspective on information need looks at all the types of human activity that require information and asks: What is the sociological context in which these information needs arise? In information seeking, needs, and uses, researchers actually do this, studying a human activity in depth but starting from the environment from which the problem, task, or other such societal-controlled information needs arise. Examples include the information needs of doctors, of lawyers, of an undergraduate researching a social science essay, or of someone seeking health information about an ailment.

All of these information needs are a result of the social roles these actors are playing. The apotheoses of this perspective on information need are the rigorous ethnographic studies done by Chatman (1996). This perspective is so specific that it is limited to substantive (Glaser and Strauss, 1967) or middle range theory-making (Boudon, 1991).

Information need considered inside the context of a problem or problem situation is a general stand-in for the multitude of human tasks that require information input from outside sources in order to be performed. For instance, a doctor treating a new patient who is complaining about an ailment must make a medical diagnosis, so this is the task needing information in order to perform it. In such research, the user's task sets the need agenda.

But the aspect of a task that requires information can also be thought of as a problem, or rather a subproblem. In other words, a task can be thought of as a series of subproblems, each of which, from the information science point of view, requires information input. In turn, this requires a decision procedure about information input. A subproblem includes 1) defining the problem with a decision procedure involving critical dimensions, 2) ranking the most critical dimensions, which further defines the problem, and finally 3) making a selection among alternative solutions (e.g., Allen and Frischmuth, 1968). This is the perspective of information science, and this is why the concept of the problem is so important to it.

But this is not what we want; it is not the essence of information need. It is too particular and it doesn't attempt to discuss (because that is not their purpose) information science concepts and link them together in relationships to form a formal theory of information need. Let's start with the notion that information need starts in the interior of the human organism.

5.2 Toward Theory: Where Information Need Starts

The information science assumption about information need outlined in the previous section rests on a logical foundation. It is not one of the primary needs: the physiological, cognitive, and affective needs that play out in our physical and social environments. Therefore, information need is not an independent or a primary human need like the need for food and water, which starts on the inside—i.e., a hunger or thirst that is internally derived. Holders of this assumption must prove that information need starts from something that occurs on the outside, in either the physical or social environment of the user.

The most typical argument is that information need results from a stimulus coming from the physical or social environment. It then enters the human sensory system. And the typical view is that our feelings or emotions are the first sensory alarm bell: that we sense or feel things first, then develop a cognitive explanation or belief that leads to information behavior. The contrary argument is that information need does not start from a stimulus to the sensory system; that information need starts when the human cognitive system is surprised or receives unexpected information from the environment. Therefore, it is not the surprising or unexpected information that starts the information need but rather the expectation of the human organism. Think of a time you were afraid. What came first, the feeling of fear or anxiety or the belief that you were afraid or anxious?

An illustrative experience occurred while I was walking down a winding road in Sheffield and seeing a truck traveling fast toward me carrying huge metal pipes coming loose from their straps. The truck passed me at high speed. But several yards past me, one of the 20-foot-long pipes burst out of the strap and bounced on the road several time before hitting a stone wall. I was not afraid in the least. I had not had time to develop a belief that I was in danger and should be afraid. We often hear of people circumventing the feeling of fear in a so-called adrenaline rush when, without having time to think, they run into a fire to save a child or pull a car door open to save a trapped family member from an imminent explosion. Or people often say when something truly eventful happens to them that "it was like being a movie." In other words, they didn't feel as if they were really experiencing it. My experience with the truck's loose pipes almost hitting me must have been similar to this. I did not believe that I was afraid so I did not act.

In Figure 5.1, we put the person's belief system, represented by the four-pronged symbol for the expectation set of possible and likely alternatives when watching a truck come down the road, into a diagram as a tentative starting position for information need to further operationalize it. If we do not have a belief that we should be fearful or feel anxious, and yet there is imminent danger, what is the information need situation? According to the previous argument, there is no information need situation. When the truck passed, the pipe flung off and hit the wall, but I had no information need.

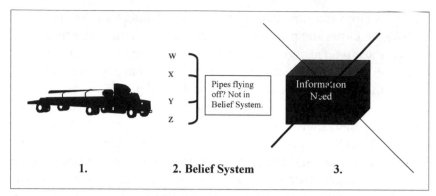

Figure 5.1   Which comes first? Belief (internal) or external stimulus?

In an information situation such as the pipe-flying incident just described, we can create a set of hypotheses about what is happening in front of us in the environment, but if it has never happened to us before—we have never experienced it—the set of all likely and possible alternatives that constitute our belief system does not include the alternative "pipes flying off." So we cannot begin the cognition leading to the formation of a belief about what is actually happening. We don't feel anything because we don't have a belief yet about what is coming at us from the environment, because we don't have a label yet to name the environmental phenomenon that we've never seen before. Therefore, there is no information need started in this potential information situation.

If we assume that information need is unknowable and nonspecifiable, to get at information need, its essence, we must resort to defining adjacent or surrogate concepts. The immediately adjacent or surrogate concepts of information need are the concept of information and information use.

CHAPTER 6

Information Use

6.1 Defining Information

We will briefly introduce the concept of information in a definitional form, then move on to information use. In the theoretical perspective of this book, they are closely associated. An operational definition of information is "by what it does" (MacKay, 1983, p. 486). According to MacKay, both semanticists and engineers define information as the effect on the human organism:

> Both mean by information that which promotes or vali-
> dates representational activity: (activity from which it is
> possible to infer something about some other state of
> affairs). Both are entitled to regard the function of infor-
> mation to be selective: to prescribe choice or decision.
> (MacKay, 1953/1955, p. 183)

As they are so tightly related in the perspective on information need taken in this book, at this point we will merge a discussion of the concept of information with the following discussion of the concept of information use.

6.2 Defining Information Use

In this book we are interested in information search, which is a specific subsection of human information behavior pertaining specifically to human utilization of an information system (Wilson, 2000). In this perspective, we place information need within a context of a user searching for information, beginning the search with an information need and ending a successful search by using the found information in some way. This is surely the goal of all information search systems and thus worth looking at more closely as a framework for getting at what information need is. Moreover, information need and information use have traditionally been associated (e.g., the *Annual Review of Information Science and Technology* chapters in the 1960s already referred to entitled "Information Needs and Uses").

If in all cases of information search, successful interaction with the information system during the search is determined by whether or not the user uses the information offered by the system, mainly in the results list, what is information use? Figure 6.1 diagrams a particular information use perspective on information need where information and information use is defined in terms of the user's selection of an alternative message from the set of all likely messages. This perspective is a receiver or user-oriented adaptation of Claude Shannon's (1949) theory of information communication between a sender and a receiver, which is influential in information needs and uses research (Herner and Herner, 1967), primarily via Donald MacKay (Buckley, 1983, p. 602). (For pitfalls in adapting Shannon, see MacKay [1983].)

Bruner (1951, p. 123) conceives of a "three-step cycle" of perception in a "tuned organism," which he defines as the organism, as a first step, beginning perception with an expectancy or hypothesis. Bruner proposed five determinants of hypothesis strength:

1. Frequency of Past Confirmation: "The more frequently a hypothesis or expectancy has been confirmed in the past, the greater will be its strength."

2. Monopoly: "The smaller the number of alternative hypotheses held by the person concerning his environment at a given moment, the greater their strength will be. ... The closer to monopoly a hypothesis is, the less information will be required to confirm it."

3. Cognitive Consequences: "The larger the number of supporting hypotheses or the more integrated the supporting system of hypotheses, the stronger the hypothesis with all that it implies for arousal, confirmation, and infirmation [disavowal]."

4. Motivational Consequences: "Hypotheses have varying consequences in aiding the organism to the fulfillment of needs. The more basic the confirmation of a hypothesis is

to carrying out a goal-striving activity, the greater will be its strength."

5. Social Consequences: "The hypothesis may be strengthened by virtue of this agreement with the hypothesis of other observers to whom the perceiver may turn." (Bruner, 1951, pp. 126–127)

Bruner's second step is the "input of information from the environment," which has certain cue characteristics; and the third step is matching the input with the organism's hypothesis (p. 124). A denied match produces internal checking for further "personological or experiential" information factors (p. 124). So-called learning occurs, leading to a revised hypothesis (Bruner, 1951, p. 124).

We diagram this preliminary conceptualization of information use in Figure 6.1. Starting from the left-hand side of Figure 6.1:

1. The expectation set is predefined by the human organism. Is the information context of the system-sender sending a signal-message to the user-receiver, which is operationalized in information theory as the set of all likely messages that could be sent? Shannon (1949) utilizes the example of the 26 letters in the alphabet as the set of all likely messages, which is an objective measure (based on past frequency of letter usage), not dependent on who the receiver is or what is expected to be received in the message.

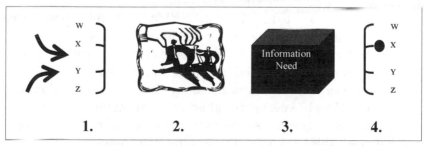

Figure 6.1 The context of information use: 1) expectation set, 2) information use defined as the user's selection from the set, and 3) information need as start position for 4) the information search routes, with "X" selected as most likely and probable

2. Is the user selecting an alternative from the set (information use)? This is an extension of Shannon, bringing in a human receiver with unpredictable expectations of what is in the message.

3. Information need, shown as a black box, is unknowable and nonspecifiable by the user in a query to an information system.

4. Start position for the information search indicates four routes of information seeking: W, X, Y, and Z, with the most likely and probable information search route "X" as the information need.

The perspective on information in Figure 6.1 is to look at the information context's effect on the human organism, defined here as the human's selection process from the predefined set of likely alternative messages that could be received in this particular information context. The selection process consists of the set of likely and possible alternative responses to the expected environmental stimulus, based on past experience with the predicted environmental object, event, or situation; the likelihood probabilities for each member of the set, based on the receiver-user's expectation of receiving each of the alternatives in the set (the probability of each alternative in the set is based on frequency calculations from past experience and is calculated in relation to the probabilities of the other members of the set). According to Langlois, "If we speak of information as involving a selection operation on the states of readiness of a system, then we can speak of the selective information-content of a signal as somehow measuring the extent or magnitude of the selection operation performed" (Langlois, 1983, pp. 592–593).

We will go quickly to the information need part of this perspective. In the just-described situation of an information system-sender sending a signal-message to the user-receiver, the expectation of the user-receiver can be explained in another way: as the state of readiness of the user to receive message alternative "W" over alternatives "X," "Y," or "Z" (or however many alternatives are in the set). The state of readiness is, in a certain sense, a way of describing this user's information need. This last part will take some explaining.

The user's state of readiness when receiving stimulus information, and whether or not, and how, the information will be used by the user, depends on how the user's prior experience and knowledge of thc system's message is organized in memory. In other words, the user's organizational structure determines how the new message (information) will be received by the user. Information use, therefore, "rearranges the structure of his or her expectations, to alter his or her states of readiness" (Langlois, 1983, p. 598). For an example of a study based on these principles in information needs and uses research, see Rosenbloom, McLaughlin, and Wolek (1965). This is a mechanistic perspective on human information use, which posits the human as an open—i.e., capable of exchanging information with the environment—and self-organizing system, which means the human information processing system is not only capable of changing, but is apt to change its structure "in response to the environment" (Langlois, 1983, p. 598).

We want to relate the information and information use diagram in Figure 6.1 directly to information need, particularly in part 2 of the figure, where we define the set and the probabilities of the set of alternatives from which the user makes the selection. The selection constitutes the use of information. The use, in turn, is dependent on the user's state of readiness to receive and use the message.

The user is in a specific *state of readiness* when utilizing an information system, a state of readiness to receive certain messages from the system more than others and certain messages less than others. The state of readiness is operationally defined by the set of likely messages the human organism is ready at that moment to receive, or expects to receive. It is from this metric that the set of alternative messages and the probabilities of each member of the set in relation to the others could, theoretically speaking, be calculated. From this analysis, information need is a function of

> the state of readiness of the human organism, operationally defined as the expectation set and the expectation probabilities of the members of the set calculated in relation to each other, and the effect on the members of the expectation set's probabilities by an environmental stimulus.

6.3 Minsky's Frame Theory

We now concretize our discussion of information, information use, and their relation to information need, via Minsky's (1975) frame theory of perception-thinking-reasoning; Minsky utilizes real-life examples to explain how humans are able to navigate through their physical and social environments. As the human organism moves "in a complex environment," it must be able to predict the environment via the formation of an "internal model of the world," but at the same time adapt to changes in the world that it has never experienced before (Arbib, 1983, p. 86). Minsky divides our internal model of the world into units called frames. A frame is a chunk of knowledge, a type of knowledge structure like a schema (Arbib, 1983; Bartlett, 1932; Piaget, 1950), but for our purposes Minsky emphasized

- How the frame creates expectations about what will be perceived in the environment based on past experience with similar environmental conditions

- How the frame receives incoming environmental stimuli

- How the frame uses the incoming environmental stimuli to adapt to the particulars of the environment in front of it at a given moment in time

Arbib further points out that a schema or frame must have within its fundamental structure the impulsion to seek out information in the environment in order to keep these representations up-to-date (1983, p. 88).

The frame for entering a room, for example, or participating in a birthday party, creates a state of readiness based on the person's past experiences with the object, event, or situation. Things that are always true about the object, event, or situation represented by the frame are at the top level of the frame, while things that are variable in the object, event, or situation are located in slots at the lower level of the frame.

Slots represent properties, elements, or dimensions of the object, event, or situation being experienced by the individual. To allow for variance in characteristics, a slot is made up of a set of all possible and likely alternatives for a property/element/dimension of the object, event, or situation. Slots are initially set to their default settings, defined as the most likely environmental signal that will be received based on frequency occurrences in the individual's past experience. However, when a stimulus is received from the environment that contradicts the default, the default can be quickly switched to an alternate setting.

Slots can encapsulate complex properties, elements, or dimensions of a frame, so that they are more like "subframes" unto themselves, with their own slots that specify conditions the assignments have to meet. As indicated in Figure 6.2, some of these assignments are shared by or at least are pointers to other related frames in the network system. According to Minsky, "this [linkage] is the critical point that makes it possible to coordinate information gathered from different viewpoints" (1980, p. 1). The linkages between all the frames and subframes via the slots means that the system is in a constant state of transformation due to the effects of new information coming into the system from the environment.

The power of frame theory is that the frame, via its slots/terminals and their default setting, creates an expectation set for that property, not just a single hypothesis. The components of the set, which is constituted based on the person's past experience with the environmental stimulus, 1) allows for quick changes in the frame based on the particular conditions of the stimuli on the day, and 2) leads to a range of carefully modulated responses to the particularities of the stimuli. An extremely sophisticated user frame, a domain-specific frame for a domain expert, for example, creates an extreme state of readiness to receive an incoming message on the topic of the expertise. In chess, for example, the chess expert can carefully modulate his or her next

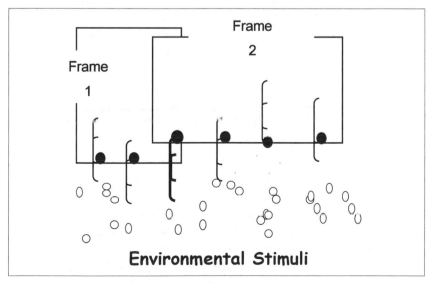

Figure 6.2   Frame, slot/terminal assignments with default setting indicated in black dot and Frames 1 and 2 sharing a slot/terminal

move depending on the play of the opposing player (Gobet and Charness, 2006).

We illustrate this conceptualization of information and information use with an example of an event from everyday life where the user is physically moving through an environment; let's say on a busy urban street. According to Minsky (1975), the person walking on the urban street has a "walking on the street" frame that is brought forward from Long Term Memory (LTM), where it is permanently stored, to the person's working memory. We will refer to this in more detail further on, but we assume that, the larger and more encompassing a frame is, the more efficient it is for the person. We further assume that, due to the frames' and subframes' flexibility, most human activity and interaction with the environment can be reasonably taken care of.

The purpose of the frame in helping a person navigate through time-space, in this case an urban streetscape going to work, can be operationalized by saying the person's perceptual/cognitive system cues from memory the appropriate urban streetscape frame that will then control the processing of incoming stimuli from the actual street. The default settings for walking along an urban street while going to work are set to the most frequent properties or dimensions of this walking situation. The frame renders the person, in effect, in "a conditional state of readiness for all possible action, including planning and evaluating action" (MacKay, 1983, p. 491).

From an information theory perspective, rather than the real or actual experience of the person walking down a street, the important thing happening is the person's continuous reception of messages from the street that permits the person to fine-tune his or her "conditional state of readiness" (see MacKay, 1983, p. 491). The fine-tuning can be as little as continuously receiving messages that confirm or give evidentiary support for what the person's mediating frame defines here as the most likely alternative, which is given the default setting. However, the rest of the members of the expectation set remain ready to be called up.

There is a set of possible and likely messages per property/dimension/element of the urban street experience, based on the person's past experience with urban street experiences. The likelihood or probability of one member of the set, per property or dimension (covering all variances in the person's past experience with the object or event currently being experienced), is calculated by the person's cognitive system in relation to all other possible alternatives for the property or dimension of the frame.

As shown in Figure 6.3, the human organism, therefore, for each slot in the frame, defined as a property or dimension of the "walking to work along a streetscape" frame, is in a constant flux of selecting and deselecting alternatives from the property set, depending on the actual circumstances of the incoming stimuli from the street. In Figure 6.3, we illustrate a person walking down the street, the person's perceptual/cognitive system continuously selecting and deselecting alternatives from the property set, in a constant quest to keep the organism's state of readiness up-to-date for its interaction with the environment. In other words, the human organism's constant selecting and deselecting of default values adapts the property or dimension to changes in the environment. The four-pronged symbol is the alternative set and the black dots are the default or selected property/element/dimension.

6.4 Adaptation: Perception

The perceptual system, as we just described it in the previous section in terms of Minsky's frame theory, is based on indeterminism—i.e., one environmental stimulus does not cause one human perceptual system effect. Only an indeterminate, or in Harnad (1987b, p. 23), an "underdetermined" human perceptual/cognitive system receiving

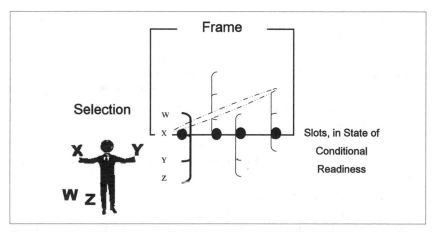

Figure 6.3   Information use and selection from a frame with slots representing properties or dimensions of the frame, each slot with a set of alternatives

information via environmental stimuli can be adequately adaptive to the inevitable surprising or novel stimulus. Humans cannot face the world each day having experienced everything, having previously seen every object, event, or situation in the world. Nor do we expect or want the physical and social environments we interact with to stay the same. In fact, as we will describe in the next section, humans are hard-wired to seek out and recognize novelty and changes in their environment. It is a human imperative, therefore, for our perceptual/cognitive system to be built for constant indeterminacy in the environment so that it can adequately update its conditional state of readiness to effectively interact with that environment. We have defined our conditional state of readiness as our expectation set. Our expectation set is, in effect, our knowledge of the world. One can say that humans are in a constant state of information need to update our knowledge of the world, our expectation set, so that we can recognize and adapt to changes in our environment. Only a continuously updated human perceptual/cognitive system enables humans to adapt effectively to the continuously changing social and physical environments in which we live.

In the case of information need for domain novices conducting an information search utilizing an information system, their knowledge about the topic, their state of readiness concerning information about the topic, and their expectation set concerning the topic must be updated for this essential adaptation to take place. Let us consider users' knowledge about the new topic to be a frame; their information need is governed by that frame. In Minsky's frame theory, there are slots at the bottom of the frame representing properties, dimensions, or elements of the overall topic frame for users, and these slots with their conditional state of readiness give the perceptual/cognitive system of individuals an adaptive propensity.

As both the computer science and information science perspective on information need are derived from Shannon's theory of communication (information), the two perspectives share this adaptive feature in their modeling of the user conducting an information search. There is an essential difference, however, which we will now describe.

The computer science perspective on the user's information need envisions a corrective or negative feedback-based adaptive system, designed to correct the error the user has made in formulating the query from his or her information need. The information need, however, is considered static.

The information science perspective, on the other hand, envisions a shifting or evolving investigation of information if the user is conducting the information search during an exploratory phase of performing a task or solving a problem. The type of feedback in the information science case is a positive feedback-based adaptive system. These two types of feedback systems are very different.

Negative feedback is a thermostat turning off when the predetermined desired temperature is achieved, then turning on and off in a continuous cycle to minimize the difference in the match between the desired and actual temperature of the room (MacKay, 1953/1955, p. 191). Negative feedback, therefore, minimizes errors in the matching between the user's actual information need and the formulation of it in the query. After viewing the system output in response to the user's first query, the user's second or revised query (i.e., query expansion, modification) is a function of this corrective procedure. The goal state of the negative feedback process is to decrease the mismatch to zero.

The positive feedback of the information science perspective, on the contrary, envisages an amplification of the environmental signal not a minimization of the mismatch between the user's information need and the query. We shall see in Chapter 7 that the amplification of an unexpected environmental signal (stimulus) via positive feedback leads to generative reasoning and knowledge formation. Information science's perspective on information need embraces positive feedback, mismatch amplification, but in this book we limit the benefit of positive feedback to only a certain kind of search. We refer to this particular type of information search as a Pre-focus, exploratory search (Kuhlthau, 1993), or an "ill-structured problem search" (Pirolli, 2007, p. 20). We define this type of search at greater length, comparing it to other types of searches, in subsequent sections of Part I.

Figures 6.4 and 6.5 illustrate the computer science and information science perspectives on information need and what happens to the need when negative and positive feedback occur. Feedback could occur at any time during the user's information search, but in this book we are mainly concerned with feedback from the results list. In Figure 6.4, for the computer science perspective on information need, negative feedback is meant to minimize the mismatch between the results list, controlled by the user's initiating query, and the user's information need. The negative feedback from the results list indicates to the user what adjustments in the query are necessary in order to achieve a better match between system output and the user's information need.

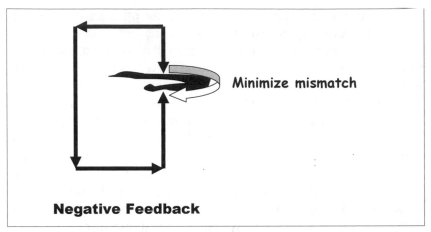

Figure 6.4   Computer science perspective on information need: negative feedback and the minimization of mismatch

In Figure 6.5, for the information science perspective on information need in an exploratory or ill-structured search, positive feedback actually maximizes the perturbation caused by the unexpected environmental stimulus signal entering the perceptual/cognitive system of the information user. The figure illustrates this with a "no expectation set." The user's perceptual/cognitive system somehow processes the unexpected signal. In Part II of this book, we give evidence from a study of the user "puzzling" over an unexpected textual stimulus, not knowing what to make of it. Eventually, a set of alternative explanations arises in the user's mind, but no alternative seems more likely than any other in the set. Nevertheless, the user is so intrigued by the information needs contained in the set that he or she conducts information searches on each of the alternatives.

In Figure 6.5, we describe information need as part of an adaptive mechanism. An unexpected stimulus signal from the environment somehow enters the perceptual/cognitive system of the user. There is very little registration of the signal. However, in information science's positive feedback conceptualization of what happens, the user's perceptual/cognitive system amplifies the perturbing signal. Knowledge formation occurs with these steps: 1) unexpected and unmatched environmental stimulus, 2) an expectation set awakens in sensory system but it is still largely undetected, 3) positive feedback maximizing perturbation of unexpected environmental stimulus signal, 4) puzzling over unexpected environmental stimulus, 5) eventually, an explanation set is produced; likely alternatives in message set given

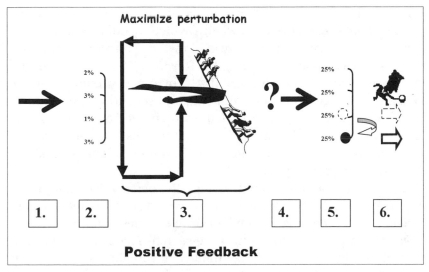

Figure 6.5   Information science perspective on Pre-focus, exploratory information search: positive feedback and maximization of perturbation via knowledge formation

equi-probabilities, and 6) information search attempted for each alternative in set.

The Shannon measure of information content produces an alternative set where the probabilities are calculated in relation to the other members of the set, rather than in absolute terms, thus increasing probabilities from number 2's "awakened" expectation set (2 percent to 3 percent range) to number 4 (equi-probabilities at 25 percent each) in Figure 6.5. The user's system puzzles over the signal, processing it to some degree, before producing a conscious explanation set for the signal, leading to new routes of information search. In effect, the knowledge system of the user—the user's conditional state of readiness—symbolized in this book by the four-pronged symbol representing the user's expectation set, has been readjusted by the system. The explanation set becomes the new expectation set, which defines the new, revised information need. The routes of information search updated by the new expectation set direct subsequent searching by the user on that topic.

We have come to the heart of the book: Information need is part of an adaptive mechanism, "merely a micro-event in a shifting adaptive process" (Hillman, 1968; quoted in Berul, 1969, p. 210). The adaptive mechanism enables the human organism to recognize unexpected stimulus signals in our physical and social environment, signals that do not fit the user's current knowledge, which we define here as his or her expectation set. "The activity of knowing is an activity of (internal) adaptive response" (MacKay, 1953/1955, p. 186), so that we continuously renew our knowledge: firstly, by our continuous need to recognize changes in the environment, and secondly by responding to changes by adapting our knowledge structures, frames, and expectation sets. Information need—the need to seek out and recognize these changes, created by unexpected stimulus signals—is at the heart of this adaptive process.

For a user of an information system, the perspective on information need, search, and information use as parts of an adaptive mechanism is a particular case. The knowledge frames of an information system user concern the topic of the search. The expectation set is established by these knowledge frames. A domain novice user has unformed, even misinformed frames, which require major adaptation. The topic patterns in this user's internal representations of the topic in his or her frames and expectation sets should not match the topic patterns the user sees in the textual environment while conducting an information search, particularly in the results list. There should be a continuous stream of unexpected textual stimuli entering the user's sensory system, which do not match the user's expectation sets. Domain novice users in particular must be driven by their information need to constantly seek out and recognize these changes from what they expected to find—patterns in the textual environment that do not match their internal representations of the topic for which information is being sought.

Figure 6.5 marks a key juncture in this book about information need. We now enter the realm of the information science concern for what information need is and how it works when an unexpected signal occurs in the environment, which is at the heart of Pre-focus, exploratory searching; at the heart of overcoming the barriers to information use for disadvantaged groups in society; and at the heart of the trend toward which mobile information accessing technology is taking us: ubiquitous exercising of our information need to conduct spontaneous information search.

We will now examine the concepts shown in Figure 6.5 in greater detail, posing the question about Step 3: Where does the internally generated new information come from to produce the revised expectation set in Step 5?

CHAPTER 7

Adaptation: Internal Information Flows and Knowledge Generation

In this chapter we give an overview of the information flow and knowledge generation processes that occur during the human perceptual/cognitive system's adaptation to receiving an unexpected stimulus signal from the physical or social environment. We first give an example of a case where these internal adaptation processes occur. A Paleolithic era modern human wakes up in a cave, calls up her usual frame for fetching the morning water from the nearby river, but discovers when she exits the cave that there is no sun that day.

In Paleolithic times, one can imagine humans rising after a night's sleep in a dark cave. Clues such as feeling refreshed after a night's sleep cause them to instantiate their "morning frame, whose goal is fetching the day's first cooking water." Then they venture out of the cave. An eclipse casts a strange sort of light. It would be such a strange light that our Paleolithic era human would not notice it at once. Then they do notice something's off. They would puzzle over the sun's absence and come up with an explanation set, which in effect becomes the revised expectation set indicating their new information need and information search investigations. There would probably be a mythical or religious alternative in the set.

The human organism receives an unexpected stimulus signal from the environment, launching an adaptation to the signal inside the internal information-knowledge system of the person. Given this proposition, the human organism unconsciously needs more information-knowledge to begin adapting to the unexpected environmental stimulus signal it has just received. The information need drives the human to seek information until the human produces an explanation-cum-revised expectation set, an internal process involving information process, information flow, and knowledge generation. Where and how does this happen?

7.1 Circles Framework

The framework for this chapter is that information need begins from a stimulus received by the user from the environment. It begins bottom-up, but when the environmental stimulus enters the user's perceptual/cognitive processing systems, there are immediate reactions from these systems, eventually causing a top-down flow of information from the system's belief and knowledge centers. In this section of the book, we briefly map out this bottom-up and top-down information flow, but shift the main explanation of these forces to Part II of the book.

In Figure 7.1, we diagram in five interconnected circles the various levels of potential information stores, information flows, and knowledge formation activities in the person's perceptual-cognitive system. Working memory can call upon these stores to provide information in a high information content situation, which is the situation when the organism receives an unexpected environmental stimulus signal. In a high information content situation, where the possible alternatives in the set are equally probable, or close to zero probability because they are largely undetected at the conscious level, the person needs information from internal sources. It is a pre-information search stage of information need. The individual can only get the information from two places:

1. From within already-obtained information and knowledge sources stored in memory

2. From the generation of new alternatives by combining two or more knowledge frames or sections of knowledge frames together, adding a new or at least reconfigured alternative source to the system

In Figure 7.1, starting from the bottom circle, Circle 1, which is the outside environment, a stimulus signal is sent to the human organism, which receives the sense data in Circle 2, but it remains largely unconscious to the organism. For some reason, Circle 2 eventually begins to process the received sense data, attempting to categorize it according to the organism's current knowledge frames. Circle 2 is a crucial phase where the environmental (outside) stimulus begins to be transduced into the code or language of the user's (internal) perceptual-cognitive system. In Circle 3, the various frames (knowledge chunks) the organism believes are relevant to processing the unexpected environmental stimulus fully codify the signal into a form that is readable by the

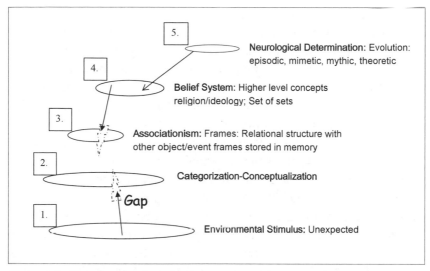

Figure 7.1 **Unexpected environmental stimulus in Circle 1 leading to a gap in Circle 2, then leading to information flowing up and down the circles, culminating in knowledge revision and/or generation**

organism's knowledge systems in Circles 4 and 5. This allows knowledge to flow down to Circle 3 where we make the assumption that most of the information processing and knowledge generation occurs. We briefly describe each of these circle levels in the following sections of Part I, and supply further explanations and illustrations of the information flow and knowledge generation in the circles in Part II.

7.2 Circle 1 to Circle 2

The start of an information need in this book is assumed to be bottom up. Information need is part of an adaptive mechanism that enables humans to react to changes in a person's physical (or social) environment. This adaptive conceptualization of information need has a long history in information science (Berul, 1969; MacKay, 1969; Taylor, 1968). According to this conceptualization, information need is stimulated into formation by the human organism receiving an unexpected environmental signal, with, however, some information content that is of use to or "interests" the human organism.

The human organism receives the unexpected environmental signal in Circle 2, where the signal registers in the individual's sensory
system; but because it does not conform to the person's current processing frame, or any existing processing frame in the person's per-
ceptual/cognitive system, the registration is at an unconscious or
barely conscious level. Figure 7.2 places Circles 1 and 2 inside the
positive feedback amplification process that an unexpected stimulus
is subjected to, which we introduced in Chapter 6 (see Figure 6.5).

In Figure 7.2, the unexpected signal from Circle 1, the environment, registers in Circle 2, the human sensory system, activating an
expectation set of which the person is not conscious. The registration
of the signal's information content produces barely noticeable probability readings in the registration expectation set, in the 1 to 3 percent range. Circle 2 must begin to process these low readings, to
amplify these readings via positive feedback, which evokes an eventual infusion of information and knowledge generation from Circles
3, 4, and 5. The sensory system begins to do this by trying to find out
what the unexpected environmental stimulus is—i.e., its meaning.
The perceptual system does this by first categorizing it.

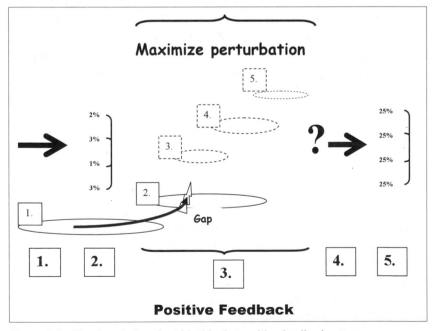

Figure 7.2   The five circles placed inside the positive feedback process

7.3 Circle 2 to Circle 3: Categorization to Conceptualization

In Harnad's (1987a, 1987b) categorical perception theory, humans begin processing an environmental stimulus by categorizing it. Humans categorize stimuli in terms of past experience with the object, event, or situation, or even, when reading text, "an abstract idea such as goodness or truth" (Harnad, 1987b, p. 1). It is believed that certain basic categories like face or color recognition are innate and do not have to be learned. These innate categories assist in the categorization of new and unfamiliar stimuli, forming the basis for humans to generate new categories via experience. The formation of new categories and the adaptation of old ones to changing conditions is a basic feature of human categorization.

In our model (Figures 7.1 through 7.5) of information flow during positive feedback and amplification of the environmental stimulus signal, categorization takes place in Circle 2. Categorization identifies what the environmental stimulus is. Circle 2 must also begin the conceptualization process of the category, which is only competed in Circle 3. Categorization can be seen as a perceptual system activity (Bruner, 1957), while conceptualization is a cognitive system activity. Conceptualization can also be seen as the cognitive system labeling the category in terms of its own symbolic language. Full conceptualization of the initiating environmental stimulus, according to Harnad (1987a), takes place only when the concept is inserted into the person's symbolic system. In our model shown in Figure 7.3, this is Circle 3.

Circle 3 is represented in Figure 7.3 as an Association Wheel. We utilize this term throughout Part II of the book, but introduce it here. It represents the association network of chunks of knowledge or frames in the person's mind. In the case of a user of an information system researching a particular topic, the person's symbolic system is an internal representation of the target topic space, a conceptual system utilized as a stand-in for the real or represented world (Arbib, 1983; Hirtle and Heidorn, 1993). The user's internal conceptual system may not be appropriate, or only barely appropriate and in need of revision. The person's representation of the world divided up into object representations, event representations, situation representations, and abstract idea representations has been investigated under various names in addition to Minsky's frame theory, including: schemas (Bartlett, 1932; Piaget, 1950), mental models, cognitive

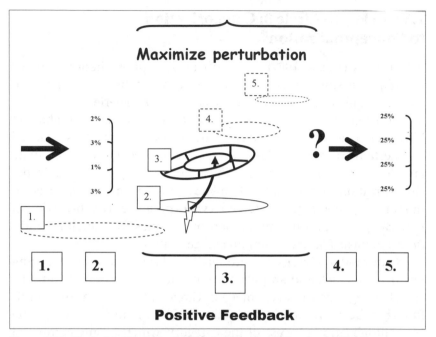

Figure 7.3 Circle 2 to Circle 3: positive feedback and signal amplification—
categorization and conceptualization of the environmental
stimulus signal

maps, concept maps, and mind maps (Cole, Lin, Leide, Large, and Beheshti, 2007).

In the five-circles conceptualization of the information flow and knowledge generation during the construction of a person's information need when an environmental stimulus cannot be processed by the person's current frames or expectation sets, Circle 3 is the symbolic system of the individual composed of a network or networks of frames, and where the generation of new frames to handle unexpected stimuli takes place.

7.4 Circles 4 and 5

Circles 4 and 5 have less evidence for what they are and for their involvement in the construction of information need than Circles 1–3. We propose them in this book because they represent in some fashion the logical notion that there are overarching systems that control information need formation in Circles 1–3. In addition, Circles 4 and 5 provide an information need perspective on recent multidisciplinary research in evolutionary psychology that attempts to get at the fundamentals of human behavior, and to create useful theories and models from these fundamentals. Elsewhere, we have started to utilize evolutionary psychology models and theories to explore the fundamentals underlying human information behavior, which is an outlook heretofore missing in information science research (Cole, 2008; Spink, 2010; Spink and Cole, 2006, 2007; see also Pirolli, 2007).

Circle 4 represents the person's belief systems, which overarch the frames in Circle 3. Circle 5 represents the person's neurological reasoning apparatus, the cognitive architecture that structures thinking and reasoning. Contrary to Circles 1, 2, and 3, information, reasoning processes, and knowledge flows downward from Circles 4 and 5. We illustrate this downward flow to Circle 3 in Figure 7.4.

7.5 Circle 4: Belief System

Circle 4 represents the person's belief system(s). These could be religious, political, gender-based, and so forth. But the belief system

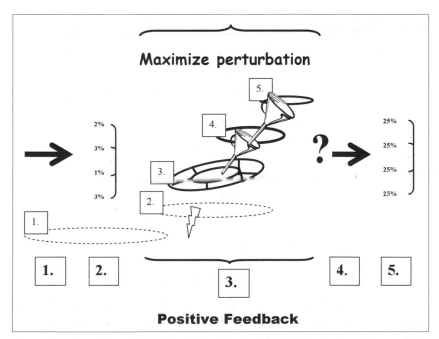

Figure 7.4 Circle 4 and Circle 5: information and knowledge flowing downward to Circle 3

represents something more fundamental as well. It covers what people believe to be true about the fundamentals of the world, even regarding such things as what constitutes a straight line or what constitutes the color red. People say: That is a straight line. Or, the coffee shop is next to the grocery store. When they really mean to say: I believe that is a straight line. Or, I believe the coffee shop is next to the grocery store. It is even said that belief comes before human feelings. That is, we have to believe we are sad, we love, we hate, before we can actually feel these things.

The person's belief system infuses the knowledge chunks or frames contained in Circle 3 with a perspective on the environmental stimulus that is being processed. It also provides cohesiveness not only to the processing of the environmental stimulus but also to the frames in Circle 3 that do the bulk of the processing work on an environmental stimulus. A belief system, in effect, gives a unity of perspective to the person's inner representation of the outer world.

Regarding information need, information flow, and knowledge generation, we highlight two aspects of Circle 4's belief system(s):

1. A belief system can serve to keep out new, novel information (Bruner, 1951; Rokeach, 1960). A belief system creates "noise" that degrades the information flow between person A, the sender, and person B, the receiver. An example is a belief system based on a prejudice. A person from the target prejudice group trying to communicate valuable information to the prejudiced person is ignored to the detriment of the prejudiced person. Groups who are the target of prejudice, on the other hand, can form their own "small world." Chatman (1996) describes the "small world" of janitors who deliberately keep out information from outsiders even though that information might be of value to the janitors.

2. A belief system can serve to let in new, novel information from the environment that would not have been recognized without the belief system.

Supported by data from an empirical study, we elaborate on the first aspect of belief systems in Part II of the book. Here, referring to evolutionary psychology research, we emphasize the second aspect only: how a belief system(s) can influence information need formation to facilitate recognition of changes in the environment, thus enabling adaptation to these changes.

Evolutionary psychology considers humans noticing novelty in the environment, adapting to these changes, and as a result creating a more competitive human organism. The role of human belief systems in this adaptation is the focus of Lewis-Williams and Pearce's (2005) recent research on the shift of humans from foraging to agriculture and the start of the Neolithic period about 10,000–14,000 years ago.

The traditional hypothesis is that the Neolithic era and the development of agriculture practices leading to sedentary habitation patterns occurred first as a result of human adaptation to climate change. This was followed, according to this traditional hypothesis, by mythological practices developed by the elite as a method of preserving social order and control in the agriculture villages. Based on the research of Cauvin (2000), Lewis-Williams and Pearce developed the contrary thesis that the Neolithic era and agriculture development started because humans saw the growing of cereals and the raising of domesticated livestock as a means to realizing their mythological or cosmological need to seek out mythological meaning via communication with the dead. These communications required the building of elaborate tunnels and stone temples such as those, first at Gobekli Tepe, then Jericho, but also Stonehenge; hence the need to remain stationary in one place. Agriculture, according to this new thesis, was in response to this human mythological need to stay in one place to build these elaborate stone and tunnel communication channels to the dead.

The elaborate and powerful belief systems of these early modern humans—the huge stone vestiges of these Neolithic structures still remain with us today—enabled these humans to change their way of looking at the world. The new perspective changed the knowledge frames of these individuals and consequently their information needs. Engineering problems regarding the transportation of the 20-foot-high stones, astronomy problems regarding the proper positioning of the large stones in relation to the sun rising, the moon, and solstices— all these new problems required information to solve them.

7.6 Circle 5: Neurologically Derived Adaptation

A supporting thesis to the previous section is Donald's (1991) thesis that roughly 30,000 years before the Neolithic era, in the Upper Paleolithic era, the human brain evolved compared to the brain of the Neanderthals, which allowed modern humans to adapt and survive changing environmental conditions while the Neanderthals could not. The primary evolutionary "culture" in this regard is the development of the "mythic culture," which is, according to Donald, a stage in the evolution of human cognitive architecture.

Donald divides the evolution of the architecture governing human thinking and reasoning into a total of four "cultures" that signify different "representational strategies" (Donald, 1991, p. 149). A representational strategy is how humans, the Neanderthals, even apes and other animal species, internally represented and thought about external reality and their place in that reality. Both the Neanderthals and modern humans share what Donald labels "episodic culture" and "mimic culture" cognitive architecture development—the ability to, respectively, conceptualize experience in terms of events or "episodes," and to act out, playback, or "mimic" occurring events or situations to others at a later time.

The evolution of the modern human brain to a "mythic culture" stage of evolutionary development separated human from Neanderthal brain development. Mythic culture is the relationship of humans to the universe in an existential sense (i.e., more than just a physical sense). (The fourth and final evolutionary stage of human brain development was to the "theoretic culture," which includes the ability to think analytically, paradigmatically, and logico-scientifically.) (For further details on Donald's thesis, cf. Cole, 2008.) This new cognitive architecture endowed modern humans with the ability to mentally represent the world in an entirely different way, thus facilitating human adaptation to changes in the environment. The Neanderthals did not share this brain development stage and consequently, according to the Donald thesis, were not able to survive.

Donald defines mythic culture as "the construction of conceptual 'models' of the human universe" (Donald, 1991, p. 213). What is the relationship of humans to such fundamental issues as the reasons for the world's creation and the concept of death? Myths are stories that explain or place humans in the wider context of the physical universe, which includes relating the present day situation of the group to past and future time. Mythic culture required or was dependent on elaborate belief frames or knowledge structures that could produce "generative modeling"—i.e., the conceptual modeling of the human universe or existence inside the objective or physical environment (Donald, 1991, p. 213). Though the "theoretic culture" developed after the "mythic culture" in the evolutionary timeline, the mythic culture strategy of representing reality remains in the cognitive architecture of the present day human brain; this is particularly evident, Donald states, in the "collective mind" of our species, "at least in the realm of social values" (Donald, 1991, p. 268). Donald makes the assumption that in fact all three previous cultures (episodic, mimic, and mythic) remain fully functional in the present day human cognitive architecture as "fully functional vestige[s]" (Donald, 1991, p. 269).

We will briefly explore Donald's "vestiges" assumption in terms of this book's overall perspective that information need is part of an adaptive mechanism. There are at least these four, let us call them "levels" of separate thinking mechanisms, so there is a level conceptualization of neurological brain architecture.

We do not know how human thinking, and particularly the role of information need as an adaptive mechanism, is determined. However, evolutionary psychology's analysis of our cognitive evolution, particularly what distinguishes our thinking from other species like the Neanderthals, gives us some clue as to how the brain is structured, how information need is formed, and the adaptive mechanisms that take place in our thinking as a result of the cognitive processes set off by information need.

In Figure 7.5, we create a conjectural diagram of Circle 5, setting out the neurological determinism underlying our five-circles conception of information need formation and its role as an adaptive mechanism. Conceptualizing Circle 5 with only Donald's culture levels is figurative only, but there is reason to hypothesize that a level conceptualization of human cognitive architecture, from an evolutionary psychology perspective, may be correct. Besides Donald's four cognitive cultures as separate levels, other evolutionary psychologists have thought of the evolution of human cognitive architecture in terms of levels. We refer specifically to Wynn and Coolidge (2004), who hypothesize about working memory.

According to Wynn and Coolidge, Long Term Memory (LTM) storage is the repository for human knowledge, but knowledge chunks or frames are called up when they are cued for by environmental stimuli, and they operate during processing in working memory. Wynn and Coolidge state that during this processing period there are multiple

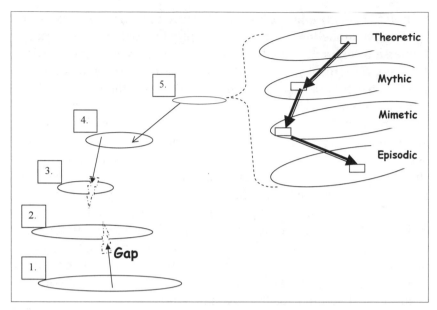

Figure 7.5 An evolution in human cognitive architecture, creating an adaptive human response to unfamiliar environmental input

retrieval structures in working memory at the same time, offering alternative retrieval/solution possibilities to the most probable hypothesis (based on past experience) for the problem or cue at hand (Wynn and Coolidge, 2004; see also Conway, Cowan, and Bunting, 2001; Duncan, Emslie, Williams, Johnson, and Freer, 1996; Kane, Bleckley, Conway, and Engle, 2001). We have consistently utilized this alternative set approach throughout the book to indicate the adaptive nature of information need, operationalized throughout by the four-pronged symbols. And the alternative set approach, we believe, stems from the most basic fundamentals of Circle 5's neurological reasoning architecture.

From the point of view of being able to recognize and adapt to novelty or changes in the environment, we underline the importance to modern humans of their hard-wired ability to retrieve from LTM and to hold in working memory multiple response solution/structures to a problem at hand. In Figure 7.5, we give Donald's four cognitive cultures as only an exemplar for this multiple set response mechanism (each culture is able to supply at least one alternative set, and from different angles, to the stimulus processing at hand). Because of the evolution in human cognitive architecture, with the evolution of the human neurological structure signified in Donald's mythic culture, modern humans were now able to keep in mind an association of elements from the different solution structures, producing the potential for a "profound interweaving of multiple tendencies that give human nature the plasticity and persistence it demonstrates" (Eigen, 2007, p. A22). The interweaving of multiple solution structures being held in working memory created a totally different thinking dynamic and advantage for modern humans over their Neanderthal competitors, because it permitted generative or new knowledge (frame) formation—new frames and new expectation sets that could not only explain unfamiliar environmental stimuli but also enable adaptation to these changes in the environment via new information needs.

CHAPTER 8

A Theory of Information Need

In this final chapter of Part I, we propose a theory of information need. The theory of information need relies on the argumentation that comes before it in Part I, but it also adds information about information need, citing additional information science research. The theory is consistent with the overall dialectic of the book, anchoring our analysis of information need in both the computer science and information science perspectives (for a modified version of this chapter, see Cole, 2011).

The dialectic between computer science and information science is shown in Figure 8.1 (the upper half is the computer science perspective; the bottom half information science's perspective). In Figure 8.1, we place Chapter 8's theory of information need inside the circles representation of information need in Part I (see Figures 7.2, 7.3, 7.4, and 7.5). The information need symbol in the chapter you are about to read is the large "V" labeled, going downwards: Q4, Q3, Q2, and Q1. The Q1–Q4 labels represent Taylor's (1968) four-level approach to information need, around which this chapter and the theory of information need is structured. As shown in the upper half of the figure, computer science's command perspective on information need is governed by a negative feedback orientation, while in the lower half of the figure, information science's question perspective on information need is governed by a positive feedback orientation.

As indicated in Part I, information need is one of the most essential concepts in information science, but it is a misunderstood concept, frequently being interpreted to mean either

A. Empirical studies of a user group's frequency of use, preference for, or satisfaction with "channels" (sources) of information, as in a needs assessment study (Kunz, Rittel, and Schwuchow, 1977, pp. 10–11; for an example, see Menzel, 1966; see also Case, 2007, p. 149); or

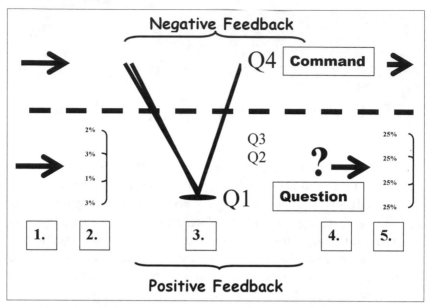

Figure 8.1   Linking Part I to Chapter 8's theory of information need

    B. A user's command to an information system (Taylor,
       1968; Jansen and Rieh, 2010)

But it is not only this. It is a much more interesting, complex concept that has intrigued information scientists for decades. The basis
of the complexity is that information need is rooted in a paradox.
Unlike the need for food, water, or shelter, or any of the other primary
human needs, what is required to satisfy the information need is
often not known to the individual concerned. And there is a question
as to whether it is a primary human need at all, but rather only a secondary need, and must therefore be contextualized in the user's situation in order to be meaningful (Wilson, 1981; Shen, Tan, and Zhai,
2005). Ironically, while most research on information need concerns
the user-centered concept, this research is largely ignored by the
computer scientists designing current information retrieval (IR) systems (Saracevic, 2007; Jansen and Rieh, 2010).

8.1 The Structure of This Chapter

This chapter starts from the paradoxical position that information
need, which is the starting position for all user information search, is

intangible and visceral and thus unknowable and nonspecifiable in a query to an information system (see most notably, Belkin, Oddy, and Brooks, 1982a). We operationalize this intangibility utilizing Taylor's (1968) classic four-level theory of information need, specifically his conceptualization of level Q1, the unconscious, visceral information need, which the user cannot know and therefore cannot specify to an IR system (for the importance of Taylor's concept of information need to information science, see Van der Veer Martens, 1999). The chapter treats information need as a form of black box, to both the user who is formulating a query to an information system and the researchers who wish to study why individuals seek information.

The most substantial portion of the chapter examines eight information science concepts or behaviors that, because of their adjacency to the concept, comment on or are a surrogate for information need. (Information use has often been associated with information need to the point where the two concepts seem almost to merge [see particularly, Lipetz, 1970].) In Figure 8.2, information need is at the figure's center as a black box, as something we cannot know, we cannot observe, and the user cannot define. Around the black box, Figure 8.2 categorizes and lists the eight concepts, grouping them into three broad categories:

1. Information Behaviors (i.e., information need is analyzed in terms of the Information Behaviors that it initiates)

2. Context (i.e., information need is produced in users by the context in which users find themselves)

3. The Human Condition (i.e., a holistic approach to information need that defines the need for information as fundamental to the human condition)

Within these three broad categories, this chapter briefly outlines the eight adjacent/surrogate concepts, one after the other, according to the numbering scheme given in Figure 8.2. The focus of each concept description, however, is on its relationship to developing a theory of information need and is therefore not a complete description. Throughout the chapter, we leave the surrogate/adjacent concept descriptions to create six propositions for the developing theory, in sections we call "Toward Theory." These propositions form the core of the theory. The theory is expressed in a summary of these propositions and two diagrams at the end of the chapter.

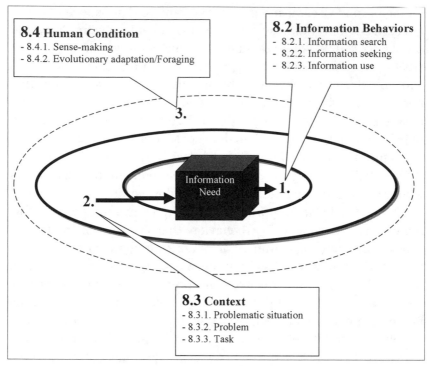

Figure 8.2 Information need as a black box, and three categories of information need surrogates

8.2 Information Behaviors

8.2.1 Information Search

The essence of information search, compared to the broader concepts of information behavior and information seeking, is that the user must formulate a query or question to an information system to make the system work. Formulating the query requires a specific mindset in the user. The user must somehow 1) collect his or her thoughts on the information that is needed, 2) identify and label these thoughts with concept terms, then 3) forecast which keywords will obtain a results list and citations to the needed information, information that will satisfy the information need. Taylor and user-oriented researchers since then (Belkin, Oddy, and Brooks, 1982a, b; Hjørland, 2010) have found that, due to the intangible and nonspecifiable nature of information need, the user formulates the query incorrectly.

To correct this initial user error in information search, Taylor theorized that the information system (librarian or IR system) must negotiate the question from the compromised expression of the need, which Taylor calls level Q4, through the Q3 formal expression of the need, to the Q2 level which is the conscious "within brain description of the need" (Taylor, 1968, p. 182). The deepest Q1 level of the need, however, is, as Taylor claimed, "visceral" (i.e., instinctual) and therefore cannot be reached in this negotiation process (though it is "traceable") (Taylor, 1962, p. 392). The main point of Taylor (1968) was to provide a strategy of question negotiation, called the five-filters tool, which gives the information system a methodology for drilling down through the user's information need levels from Q4 to Q2.

8.2.1.1 Information Search: The Query

The query is a key concept for system-oriented IR system designers; it is the starting event upon which the remainder of the conceptual apparatus of IR rests (Jansen and Rieh, 2010). But system-oriented IR system designers treat the query as a given, the user command that commences the system's work of matching the symbols that make up the query with symbols in the index system for the content stored in the system's database. Jansen and Rieh (2010) describe the system view of the query as: "a set of one or more symbols that is combined with other syntax and used as a command for an information retrieval system to locate possibly relevant content indexed by that system" (Jansen and Rieh, 2010, p. 1528). What underlies the user's formulation of the query is not considered important in the traditional, system-oriented model.

Taylor himself was aware of this disconnect and confronted it head on in Taylor (1968), where he analyzed the disconnect in terms of commands versus questions:

> Let us discuss briefly *commands* and *questions*, for an understanding of the difference between them is critical for the development of truly interactive systems. (Taylor, 1968, p. 188; emphasis in original)

In Taylor's view, the traditional, system-oriented query-as-a-command conceptualizes the user-system transaction as a "known answer" (or a known form of the answer) finding system. In Taylor's words: "A command basically denotes the request for a specific item or specific subject combination which the inquirer has already assumed will satisfy his need" (Taylor, 1968, p. 188). A question, on the other hand, assumes that the user does not know either the answer or the form of the answer.

Taylor constructed a four-level model of information need in order to join together in a coherent whole both the command perspective and question perspective on the user query. The Q4 top level is the command level while the deeper Q1, Q2, and Q3 levels are the question levels. It was the desire to reconcile and join together these two perspectives that animates Taylor's (1968) article. Taylor, however, is not talking about two types of information need, a command-type of information need and a question-type of information need, but rather two types of information search:

1. A command-type of information search means that the user "knows exactly what he wants and can describe its form (book, paper, etc.) and its label (author and title)" (Taylor, 1968, p. 191); in response to the command, "the inquirer is delivered a specific package," which, "by definition," satisfies the inquirer (p. 188). In information science, this type of search is referred to as a Known Item Search (Cutter, 1904). We will add here another search type but of the same genre, called the Known Answer or Form of Answer Search. This is a search where the user knows exactly what type of answer or what the form of the answer is. It has even been argued that this type of subject/topic search is in fact a form of known item search (Bates, 1998, p. 1186).

2. A question-type of information search means that the user is questioning the system not knowing the answer or the form of the answer to be received from the system, called an Unknown Item or Unknown Answer (or form of the answer) Search. Other labels for this type of search are "exploratory," "ill-structured problem," and "subject or topic search" (Lee, Renear, and Smith, 2006; Meadow, Boyce, Kraft, and Barry, 2007; Pirolli, 2007). Here, the user only knows "fringes of a gap in knowledge," making it extremely difficult for users to identify and describe the information gap or need (Bates, 1998, p. 1186; see also Belkin, Oddy, and Brooks, 1982a; Borgman, 2000), so they cannot identify an effective start state from which to form a query and to utilize an information system. For a

complete description of types of searches, see Cole, Julien, and Leide (2010).

The two broadly described search types coincide with what we call the Vertical Interpretation of Taylor: that every user query has Taylor's four levels of information need, but there are the just-described command- and question-based types of searches. The phase or Horizontal Interpretation of Taylor's model, where the user goes through Q1 to Q4 in four phases of performing a task or solving a problem, is described in the next section.

8.2.1.2 Toward Theory: Proposition 1

We label the two different interpretations of Taylor's four-level model of information need the Vertical Interpretation and the Horizontal Interpretation. The Horizontal Interpretation or phase approach to Taylor, however, is easier to understand and seems to be the predominant view (see Hjørland, 2010, p. 222). Belkin (1980, p. 136) utilizes the word "stage" to describe Taylor's levels even though Belkin's ASK is a Vertical Interpretation of Taylor (see Belkin, 1980, p. 137). According to Hjørland, for example, "'information need' progresses in a relatively independent fashion 'inside the head' of the user; it develops continuously and goes through the phases Q1, Q2, Q3, and Q4 ... " (Hjørland, 2010, p. 222). The last Q4 phase, according to this Horizontal Interpretation, is when the user approaches an IR system. The user knows the answer or form of the answer he or she wants the system to find, so the user issues a command to the information system. Accordingly, users can easily express their information need to the IR system (Nicolaisen, 2009; for the assumptions underlying this view, see also Dervin, 2003a, pp. 326–327). (Support for the Horizontal or phase Interpretation in Taylor [1968] is the word "stage" in Taylor's description of the Q2 level [p. 182, column 2].)

However, the overwhelming evidence in Taylor (1968) is that his model requires a Vertical not a Horizontal Interpretation. Taylor sets out the traditional system-oriented model of the user, criticizing its assumption that the user's query is a command to an answer-finding system rather than a question. Further evidence for the Vertical Interpretation is the importance Taylor gives to Q4 level being the "compromised expression of the need," the article title which highlights the phrase "question-negotiation," and the space devoted in the abstract to his five-filters question-negotiation technique for drilling down from the Q4 compromised-need level to the Q2 conscious level of the user's information need (see also Saxon and Richardson, 2002):

> Within this context, the *question*, as contrasted to the command, can be better understood. … the command is Q4, the question compromised by the rigidities of the system … However, the *question* moves back toward Q3 and even toward Q2. (Taylor, 1968, p. 189; emphasis in the original)

Because we feel the level or Vertical Interpretation is so essential for Taylor's insight into what information need is, we put the Vertical Interpretation in a propositional form:

> **Proposition 1:** As per Taylor's model, there are no command-only type information needs. Rather, there are different types of searches, some of which have a command intention (to obtain a known item or known form of an answer), and some of which have a question intention (to explore a topic area when the item or the form of the answer is unknown to the user). Both types of searches, however, are motivated by the four levels of information need.

8.2.2 Information Seeking

To illustrate the difference between a Horizontal Interpretation of Taylor and a phase approach to a user performing a task, with the same information need over all the phases but with different types of information searches that predominately occur in these different phases, we refer to Kuhlthau's (1993) six-stage Information Search Process (ISP) Model. Kuhlthau's model is actually an information seeking model but was created before Wilson (1999) determined the generally accepted distinction between information seeking (all purposive information seeking behavior) and information search (user-IR system interaction.) Kuhlthau's ISP Model is one of the most cited and useful information seeking models in information science (e.g., Ellis, Wilson, Ford, Lam, Burton, and Spink, 2002; Ford, Wilson, Foster, Ellis, and Spink, 2002; Spink, Wilson, Ford, Foster, and Ellis, 2002a; Spink, Wilson, Ford, Foster, and Ellis, 2002b; Wilson, Ford, Foster, Ellis, and Spink, 2002).

Kuhlthau's ISP Model of information seeking, outlined in Figure 8.3, describes a six-stage model of students doing a school assignment, starting from the Stage 1 Initiation stage when the student receives first notice of the project from the instructor, to the presentation of the project in Stage 6. The key stages we would like to focus on here are Stage 3 and Stage 4. In Stage 3, the students in Kuhlthau's studies have selected their school assignment topic and now must explore the topic area to formulate a focus for the assignment, which occurs in Stage 4.

The stage the student is in when seeking information has a profound effect on the type of information search students conduct when they decide to utilize an IR system. In Figure 8.3, we link Kuhlthau's six-stage information seeking model with the types of information searches discussed in the previous section. In Stage 3, the exploration stage, the student will engage in Unknown Item Search, while in Stage 5, the Post-focus collection stage, the student will engage in a Known Item Search or a Known Form of Answer Search.

While it seems intuitively obvious that the student will have different information needs over the course of doing a school project, Taylor's point is that this is not actually the case—that there will be different types of searches but that the information need remains constant. This seems counterintuitive, because a school project can last many days, weeks, even months. But what Taylor is saying, in his knowledge-information structure of information need, is that the Q1 deepest part of the user's information need, the knowledge-based part, will remain the same. The knowledge part or question levels of the student's information need when an information search is conducted is linked, in Kuhlthau's six-stage ISP Model, to the formulation of a focus for the assignment stage, Stage 4. If looked at from a broad perspective, one can see, here, the idea that all information searches for a school assignment involve the same information need because the searches should be in the service of the knowledge creation part of a school assignment or essay.

8.2.2.1 Information Seeking to Information Search: Berrypicking

For the last decade, information seeking research has sought to "inform" the overall design principles underlying information search systems, or IR systems (Wilson, 1999, p. 258). Information seeking, defined as all purposive human information behavior (Wilson, 2000), however, has a much wider mandate than the user-system focus of information search. This is because information seeking developed as a research area when information systems were made up of various

Stages	Initiation	Selection	Exploration	Formulation	Collection	Presentation
Feelings (affective)	Uncertainty	Optimism	Confusion/ Frustration/ Doubt	Clarity	Sense of direction/ Confidence	Relief/ Satisfaction or disappointment
Thoughts (cognitive)	General/ Vague			Narrowed/Clearer	Interest up	Clearer/Focused
Actions (physical)	Seeking background information		Seeking relevant information		Seeking relevant or focused information	
Information Search Type			- *Unknown Item Search*	*	- *Known Item Search* - *Known Form of Answer Searches*	

Figure 8.3 Kuhlthau's (1993) six-stage ISP Model in upper part of figure (Feelings, Thoughts, and Actions), with the bottom row containing the type of search for Stage 3, and, after the Stage 4 focus formulation, the type of search in Stage 5

subinformation systems—card catalogs, indexes and abstracts, the reference desk, and so on. In research studies of their efficacy, these sub-information systems, created by information professionals to facilitate user access to information, were considered "formal" channels of information seeking. Information seeking research, however, embraced empirical evidence that showed user preference for "informal" channels of information seeking—i.e., preference for asking questions of colleagues, family, and friends—over formal information tools and systems. Because informal channels were preferred by users for emotional and/or psychological reasons, information seeking researchers also became interested in the emotional and psychological factors underlying user selection of one type of channel over another (e.g., Line, 1971).

Bates's (1989) berrypicking model of information search is a prime example of information seeking's concern for a wide perspective on human information behavior shifting into their study of information search, a perspective which is completely different from the computer scientists' classic model of information search. Jansen and Rieh (2010) conceptualize this same distinction as an information search perspective versus an information retrieval perspective. In the classic, computer scientist model of information search, the user retains the same information need throughout the search, even when viewing the results and revising the query to improve the results list (i.e., so that the results list better conforms to the original information need). The user, according to this view, refines the query when viewing the results list, but retains the original information need (cf. also

Hearst, 1999, p. 263; Jansen and Rieh, 2010; Salton, 1968; Salton and Buckley, 1990).

Bates (1989, p. 409) states that while this single information need model is suitable for some searches, it is not suitable for all searches, "perhaps not even the majority" of searches. For these other types of searches, users berrypick pieces of information a bit at a time, think about the information they've found, partially by relating it to what they are trying to accomplish with the search (see more details later on this goal or task aspect of information search). As a result, their conceptualization of the information need changes, "in part or whole" over the course of an information search session (Bates, 1989, p. 413), giving the user "new ideas and directions to follow and consequently a new conception of the query" (Bates, 1989, p. 410).

In Figure 8.4, we illustrate Bates's shifting user conceptualization of their information need due to berrypicking during a single search session. Bates describes the user's starting position for the search as being derived from the user's information need, which she further specifies as being derived from "features of a broader topic" (Bates, 1989, p. 409). Vakkari, Belkin, and others call these features "aspects of the topic" (Vakkari, 2001, p. 54; see also Dumais and Belkin, 2005). Refer to Figure 8.3 and Kuhlthau's six-stage ISP Model for an example of where the topic figures in the performance of a task. The user does not know all of the aspects or what aspects of his or her knowledge of the broader topic area will be useful when formulating the query (Belkin, 1980, p. 139; see also Belkin, Oddy, and Brooks, 1982a, p. 63).

In Figure 8.4, the user's topic is indicated by a rectangle, and the selected aspects of the topic are indicated by circles. On the left-hand side of the figure, the user selects the aspects to form the initiating query. The user then goes through the search utilizing the IR system, berrypicking bits and pieces of information in the results list and elsewhere, contemplating the pieces of information, reconceptualizing the information need, then moving on to a different query based on a selection of different aspects. Some of the aspects (the circles in the figure) are outside the topic (perhaps indicating wasted effort). The process repeats itself continuously during the search. At the end of the search, different aspects (circles) are indicated in the topic square as constituting the user's evolved or shifted conceptualization of the information need.

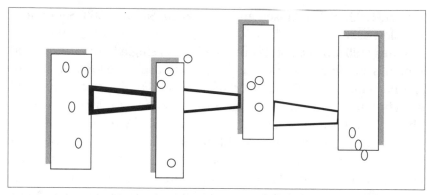

Figure 8.4   Bates's berrypicking information seeking perspective on information search for a user in Kuhlthau's Stage 3, when the user conducts information searches to explore different aspects (indicated by small circles) of the topic (indicated by rectangles)

8.2.2.2 Toward Theory: Proposition 2

We wish here to add an important nuance to Bates's berrypicking model of information search. It is not the information need itself that evolves or shifts over the course of the search, but rather the aspects of the topic the user selects to investigate that shifts or evolves over the course of the search. In Figure 8.4, it is the topic aspects the user selects to investigate that evolve or shift over the course of the search, not the user's information need. This is an important nuance that we put in propositional form:

> **Proposition 2:** When the user is in the exploratory stage of information seeking, it is only aspects of the user's information need (topic, etc.) the user selects to investigate, not the information need itself, that evolve and shift over the course of a search session.

In order for berrypicking information to have an effect on the shift and evolution of the aspects of the information need selected by the user to investigate over the course of a search session, the user must use the information in some way. In the next section we describe the different types of information use.

8.2.3 Information Use

Information use is defined by Wilson as "the physical and mental acts involved in incorporating the information found into the person's existing knowledge base" (Wilson, 2000, p. 50); these acts include reading, thinking about, note taking, diagramming, and any of the other physical and mental actions humans do to "work" information (Dervin, 1992; Ford, 2004; Todd, 1999). There are different kinds of information use effects on a user's information need during information search. During information search according to Pirolli, the effects of the physical and mental acts the user does to incorporate found information into his or her existing knowledge base may "create, elaborate, or modify [the user's information need] specification" (Pirolli, 2007, p. 65).

In information science, information use is firmly linked to information (versus an objective notion of information, e.g., Shannon, 1949), which Brookes (1980, p. 131) defined in his "fundamental equation of information science" ($K[S] + ¢I = K[S + ¢S]$) as "that which modifies a user's knowledge structure." Information and knowledge in his equation are measured in the same units and are therefore "of the same kind" (Brookes, 1980, p. 131). Essential to this information definition is that new data or stimuli from the environment interact with the user's pre-existing knowledge about the topic, which is stored in packets or clumps of knowledge called knowledge structures, schemata, frames, or mental models. To illustrate the creation, modification, and elaboration of a new knowledge structure when a user conducts an information search in a new topic area, we briefly refer to Minsky's (1975) frame theory.

Minsky argued that human perception is made up of a sequential series of discrete, perceptual events; it is an "illusion" that it seems continuous and organized (Minsky, 1975, p. 221). The analogy is to a movie on film where the action seems continuous but is actually made up of thousands of separate frames turned quickly by the movie projector so that the human eye views it as one. In perception, central to this illusion of continuity is that humans perceive and "use" incoming environmental stimuli via prepackaged frames, created from previous experience with objects and events. These prepackaged frames process incoming stimuli; and once the perceptual/cognitive system labels the stimuli, and brings forth from memory the appropriate frame, the frame predicts what the person is experiencing at the moment, and thus creates the appearance of continuity of perception. Minsky gives the example of a room-object.

For a person who has never experienced a room, they have no room frame stored in memory and therefore cannot effectively use the stimuli they receive when entering a room, any room, for the first time. The person's frame system, however, has an "information retrieval network" which supplies a beginning frame from adjacent spheres of this person's experience stored in memory (Minsky, 1980, p. 2). "These inter-frame structures," Minsky (1980, p. 2) states, "make possible other ways to represent knowledge about facts, analogies, and other information useful in understanding" the actual room being experienced. We will call this "borrowing" a frame. With constant experience of rooms, however, the person will build a room-frame, with default settings for prototypical rooms so that the person can predict what he or she will find when entering a new room, and with terminal settings that allow for the illusion of continuity as the person's gaze shifts around the new room. The default settings allow the person to adapt the room frame to the actual room being experienced.

Minsky's frame theory creates a limited taxonomy of the information use types involved when an information system user, new to a topic area and who is in Kuhlthau's exploratory stage (Stage 3 of the ISP) of information seeking, incorporates found information into his or her knowledge base:

- Use Type 1: This user "borrows" a frame for the new topic based on analogies and knowledge from adjacent topic areas stored in memory. This leads to berrypicking information while the user selects and investigates a continuously shifting or evolving series of aspects of the new topic.

- Use Type 2: At a certain point, focus formulation occurs (in Stage 4 of the ISP), the new topic actualizes its own frame, and the frame's default slots and terminals become filled in.

- Use Type 3: Subsequently, the user allows for a more efficient type of information search (for further description of this process, see Cole, 1994b, 1998).

We label these three different types of information use by reducing Kuhlthau's six-stage ISP Model (following Vakkari, 2001) to Pre-focus information use, Focusing information use, and Post-focus information use.

In Figure 8.5, we diagrammatically represent these three stages of information seeking, divided according to the three different types of information use indicated in the previous paragraph. The left-hand

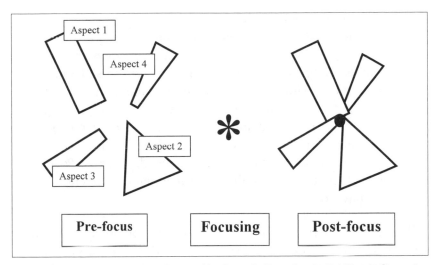

Figure 8.5 Pre-focus information seeking/search, Focusing in Kuhlthau's Stage 4, and Post-focus information seeking/search (right-hand side of figure) in Kuhlthau's Stage 5

side of the figure represents Stage 4, the exploration stage of information search when the user investigates different aspects of the topic; the middle asterisk indicates the actualization of the new topic frame, and the creation of the terminals, slots, and defaults of the new topic frame. In the Post-focus stage, information search with an information system is governed by a fully formed information need frame (Stage 5).

8.2.3.1 Toward Theory: Propositions 3 and 4

In Figure 8.6, we relate these three types of information use to Taylor's four-level model of information need. In (a) the Pre-focus stage, because the information need frame is not yet actualized, the user investigates aspects of the topic to build up the topic frame, utilizing Q4 compromised need queries in the information system. During (b) the Focusing stage, the actualization of the user's frame is achieved by the user connecting or hooking the user's Q4 information search to the Q1–3 question levels of the information need. This enables the user, in (c) the Post-focus phase, to send Q4 commands to the IR system, thus utilizing the highly efficient Known Item and/or Known Answer or Form of Answer information search. We specify this as the third proposition of our developing theory of information need:

Proposition 3: Information use evolves as the user's information seeking progresses through the Pre-focus,
Focusing, and Post-focus stages. The user begins a new
topic search (pre-focus) utilizing a Q4 compromised information need, with the queries not connected to the deeper
Q1, Q2, and Q3 levels of the information need. In Focusing
stage, the user's information need frame is actualized and
the query becomes connected to the deeper, Q1, Q2, and
Q3 levels of the user's information need. Then in Post-
focus stage, the user is able to utilize highly efficient Q4
command queries to the IR system.

Figure 8.6 illustrates an information seeking perspective on information search. Such a perspective is a very different vision of information search than the present computer science designed systems,
which assume users send command or answer-finding commands to
the system rather than questions to the system. A command IR system assumes the user either knows the answer or knows the form of
the answer before sending the command. The information seeking
perspective, on the other hand, assumes the user's need for information is based on formulating questions and asking questions based
on an information need. The information seeking perspective, therefore, starts from a different view of the user than the traditional user
model and consequently envisages a completely different information system to serve that user.

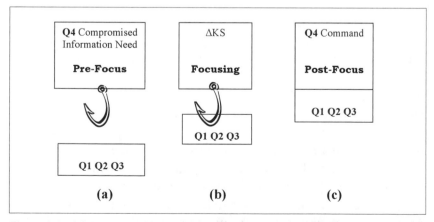

**Figure 8.6   (a) Pre-focus, (b) Focusing, and (c) Post-focus stages of the
information seeking perspective on information search**

The model of the user envisaged by the information seeking perspective and Taylor's model of the user's information need is of a user interested in knowledge structure formation and elaboration rather than an answer-focused Q4 level information accessing system. "This approach," according to Taylor (1968, p. 189), with its distinction between the Q4 level and Q1–Q3 questions levels, "may also give clues to a better understanding of the differences between information and knowledge." On the one hand is the Q4 level, which is information-search-oriented, while on the other hand the Q1–Q3 question levels are knowledge-formulation-oriented. We would like to introduce the notion here that the type of information system envisaged by the information seeking perspective is in fact a knowledge formation system rather than an IR system, which we put into a proposition:

> **Proposition 4:** The information system envisaged by the information seeking perspective is in fact a knowledge retrieval/formation system which facilitates the user formulating and elaborating an information need knowledge structure. The knowledge structure is actualized when the user links information search Q4 compromised-need commands to the deeper Q1–Q3 question levels of the user's information need.

According to Taylor (1982, p. 343), the added value of an information system is 1) to signal to the user data that have potential value to this user's information need by 2) relating this potential to the needs of the user's "specific environment" (Taylor, 1982, p. 343). With 2), Taylor shows a way forward for information system design, a way out of the impasse posed by the unknowability and nonspecifiability of the user's information need: to facilitate the user actualizing the visceral, inexpressible deepest Q1–Q3 levels of an information need by referring it to the user's specific environmental context.

8.3 Context of Information Need

In the 1980s, user-oriented researchers turned away from information need and toward the context in which the need arises. This was due to Taylor's unknowability and nonspecifiability of information need, but also because of Wilson's (1981) influential article, which stated that information need was not a stand-alone human need but rather a secondary need, dependent on the primary physiological, cognitive, and affective human needs that arise due to such things as the user's social and work roles (see also Case, 2002, pp. 73–74; Case, 2007, pp. 78–79). This broad framework was further specified in the 1990s by studying the user's task; the user's task provides a tighter, perhaps more manageable frame of reference for predicting the user's motivation for seeking information.

By contextualizing the user's information need in the user's problem situation, social and work environment, or task, an IR system (librarian or computer), it was reasoned, could get at, and implicate in the information search—so that the system could facilitate the satisfaction of the user's need—the user's primary physiological, emotional, and cognitive human needs.

8.3.1 Problematic Situation

Reacting against the unknowability and nonspecifiability of the user's information need in Taylor's model of it, which prevented the user from creating an effective query to an information system, Belkin (1980; Belkin, Oddy, and Brooks, 1982a) devised his famous Anomalous States of Knowledge (ASK) IR strategy. Later in Belkin and Vickery (1985), Belkin's ambivalence toward the concept of information need became stronger via agreement with Wilson's (1981) downgrading of information need to a secondary human need, which highlighted the sociological context where the primary human needs played out. In this influential move away from the psychological concept of information need of Taylor, the focus of research attention shifted toward the sociology of the user, specifically to the user's problem or problematic situation from which the user's information behavior arose: "The problem which the user faced was the determinative factor in producing the psychological state which leads to information behavior" (Belkin and Vickery, 1985, p. 16; see also Wersig and Windel, 1985). The user's problem is socially based. The difficulty here is to obtain both a manageable and a representative slice of the user's sociological environment, and to also include the perspective or mental mechanisms the user employs to mediate reality. For this, Belkin relies on Wersig's concept of the "problematic situation."

The problematic situation is the user's recognition that there are insufficiencies in his or her internal mental models of "her or his environment, knowledge, situation, and goals" that prevent the achievement of the desired goals; the user is alerted to these insufficiencies via "uncertainty values" (among other indices) attached to the models (Belkin and Vickery, 1985, p. 14). To attain the degree of certainty required for reasonable action, the user seeks information from outside sources. Wersig later specified reasonable action as the user being able to manage the problem, or "problem management" (Belkin and Vickery, 1985, p. 17), which requires managing both the user's internal cognitive states and the user's social roles.

8.3.2 Problem

According to Belkin, "the problem ... the user faced was the determinative factor in producing the psychological state which leads to information behavior" (Belkin and Vickery, 1985, p. 16). Belkin proposed an ASK IR system strategy which automatically modeled the anomalies in the user's conceptual state of knowledge (ASK) concerning a particular topic or situation, starting from a written problem statement. This problem statement focused on the user's problems, "what they intended to do and what they perceived as problems or difficulties" (Belkin and Vickery, 1985, p. 15). Based on the strength of the associations between concept word pairs and concept clusters in the problem statement, the ASK IR system strategy created an association map. The IR system classifies the association map, from which the IR system then derives an optimal retrieval strategy. In effect, the IR system utilizes the user's ASK structure, derived from the association map, to serve as the user's query to the IR system. If the user's ASK is resolved by the potential information provided to the user in the results list, "the user's unknown and non-specifiable information need is also satisfied even though it is never represented in the transaction between the user and IR system" (Cole, Leide, Beheshti, Large, and Brooks, 2005, p. 1546).

In Figure 0.7(a), we illustrate a hypothetical ASK as a type of information need frame that can be utilized by the IR system as a surrogate for the user's information need. The ASK is derived from an association map of the concepts the user indicates in the written problem statement, the concept relationships, and the strength of the concept relationships from the placement of the concepts in the user's problem statement. Following Belkin, Oddy, and Brooks (1982b), strong associations between concepts are shown in Figure 8.7(a) by thick solid lines, medium associations with narrow solid lines, and weak associations with dotted lines. The ASK IR strategy, when it is presented to the user during information search, is designed to jolt the user into another state of knowledge, thus affecting the user's subsequent information need concerning the user's own goals in seeking information:

> The question of use or effect of information is implicit in their [Belkin and his colleagues' ASK] research, in that the strategies for response are based on the idea of effective change in state of knowledge, in terms of the goals of the individual. (Belkin and Vickery, 1985, p. 15)

8.3.3 Task

There are advantages to utilizing the user's task as an information need frame rather than framing the user's information need in a problem. The user's perspective on his or her problem is a personal, subjective perspective (Wersig and Windel, 1985), while the user's task is largely an objective construct that explicitly considers or models the user's specific work or social role (Wilson, 1999). A sophisticated model of a doctor's task when diagnosing a patient's medical condition, for example, can be provided to the user by the IR system (Cole, Cantero, and Ungar, 2000). The task of researching and writing a legal brief is set out by professional practice, which determines the information the lawyer needs to complete it (see Cole and Kuhlthau, 2000). For a domain novice user who is in a Pre-focus stage of information seeking, a task-based IR system that follows through the procedures of the task, with opportune prompting for effective information search, has the potential to be an extremely useful surrogate information need frame until the user's own information need frame can be actualized.

We present an example of a task-based information need frame in Figure 8.7(b) which is specifically designed for an undergraduate student researching a social science essay. As in Kuhlthau's six-stage ISP Model, the undergraduate begins essay research by selecting a topic (in Stage 2) then investigating aspects of the topic in an exploratory manner in Stage 3. Unbeknownst to most undergraduates, who are domain novices, is that the topic or surface layer information search is not the essence of their task. Their real task in their research and writing is "to put their learning on display so that they will receive a high mark from the course instructor." The undergraduate's information need, therefore, is to seek information that will fulfill the task requirement of putting the student's learning on display for the instructor marking the essay by utilizing a high impact essay style such as a compare and contrast essay (Leide, Cole, Beheshti, Large, and Lin, 2007).

The diagram in Figure 8.7(b) encapsulates in visual form the parts of the social science compare and contrast essay, starting from the essay's thesis statement: "There were the same causes leading up to WWI and WWII." The two concept circles that are compared and contrasted are World War I (WWI) versus World War II (WWII). The generic relationship lines between the two concept circles are Social, Political, and Economic. These relationship lines are vehicle concepts by which the user will be able to compare and contrast the causes leading up to WWI versus WWII. The undergraduate fills out the diagram with the specific concept elements of the essay and the diagram is then used by the IR system as the user's query to the IR system. (Part III of this book illustrates this task-based IR system.)

The information need frames of problematic situation, problem, and task create containers that are designed to make the user think about his or her need in a formulaic, socially efficient way. These formulas are derived from the social and work roles of the user, which are socially taught and evaluated. For purposes of this chapter, problem and task containers inject sociological information into the user's information need frame, thus facilitating the intermixing of valuable sociological input into the psychological information need state of the user concerning the topic area for which information is being sought. Especially for a domain novice user who is not aware of the problem-solution structure of a problem, or of what her real task is, it is at this crucial point, when the individual takes in valuable input from the outside environment via a problem or task frame, that the user's information need frame is transformed, due to an information use process of the type described by Brookes's (1980, p. 131) fundamental equation.

8.3.3.1 Toward Theory: Proposition 5

In this section, we hypothesize about the role of the user's 1) problem-based ASK or 2) task in terms of Taylor's information need model. Let us assume 1) and 2) are formulas that the IR system utilizes as structuring and information need formulation frames. The IR system supplies the frame for the user to fill in with concept terms, which prompts the user to go deeply into his or her information need. But do these information need frames go all the way down to the Q1 question level of Taylor's information need model? We believe they do not, which we discuss in subsequent sections.

In Figure 8.7, we juxtapose the information need frames based on (a) Belkin's ASK structure, and (b) Cole et al.'s (Leide, Cole, Beheshti, Large, & Lin, 2007) Compare and Contrast Essay Style task-structure, indicating in (c) that these two frames hook down to the Q2 level in Taylor's four-level model of information need, but not far enough down to hook Taylor's Q1 level. Taylor's Q1 level, the user's actual, unconscious, visceral information need, remains unhooked and uninvolved. However, we propose that problem and task frames have great power:

> **Proposition 5**: Socially imposed information need frames do not hook down to Taylor's Q1 information need level but they have great power. This is because these socially sanctioned formulas structure what the user is thinking about the topic into socially approved moulds (which have shown their efficacy over time), which can induce a perspective transformation in the user, even causing the user to focus.

8.4 The Human Condition

8.4.1 Sense-Making

Dervin's sense-making approach is a broad perspective, all-encompassing information seeking theory that looks at human information behavior at both a social and existential level. Humans seek information because the world has persistent gaps—the "assumption of discontinuity," as Dervin calls it (Dervin, 2003b, p. 270), which is our "continuing human dilemma" (Dervin, 2003a, p. 332). We bridge the gaps by "construct[ing] a sense of the world and how it works" via constant information seeking (Dervin, 2003a, p. 329). On the one hand, individuals seek information to deal with gaps in the sense or understanding they have of themselves and their relationship with the outside world, as they evolve through life; on the other hand, human beings must constantly seek and use information to make sense of "an ever-changing, sometimes chaotic, sometimes orderly, sometimes impenetrable time-space" that constitutes their relationship with existence (Dervin, 2003a, p. 331). "The result is a view of humans who are themselves ordered and chaotic moving

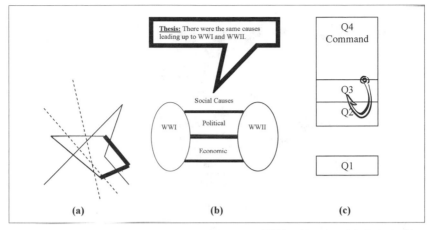

Figure 8.7   Information need frames: (a) Belkin's ASK hooking into (c) Taylor's Q2 level of information need; and the (b) Task-based frame hooking into (c) Taylor's Q2 level of information need

through a reality that is ordered and chaotic" (Dervin, 2003a, p. 330). In Figure 8.8, we illustrate Dervin's two relationships with two broken-parallel space-time lines, one representing the continuous gaps in the individual's sense of self and that individual's position in the world, with the other line representing the gaps that occur in the reality in the world outside the individual. Constant gaps require the user to constantly seek information to ascertain where the world is and to make new sense at every moment.

There is also an existential or theorizing level to Dervin's conceptualization of the human need to seek information, spurred by the "absence of complete instruction from the environment" (Dervin, Jacobson, and Nilan, 1982, p. 429). Dervin (1992, 1999) conceptualizes humans as organisms that are hardwired to theorize or "make-sense" of their environment; it is "a mandate of the human condition" (Dervin, 1999, p. 733). As a result of this sense-making imperative, humans are hardwired to continuously seek out gaps, and when they see or recognize a gap in their understanding, it automatically invokes a process of adapting their theories to making sense of the gap, to make a "new sense." This symbiotic dialogue with the world is a continuous, existential-level or macro-level quest that does not stop when the individual utilizes an information system to conduct an information search for a specific, micro-level problem or task. This existential-level quest forms part of that user's information need

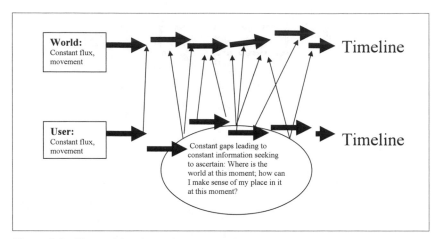

Figure 8.8   The world and user in constant flux

and, we assume, is what constitutes a major part of the deepest, Q1 question level of the information need.

8.4.2 Evolutionary Adaptation and Information Foraging

In a certain sense, as we broaden the picture on human information behavior, we go deeper into the Taylor information need levels. Evolutionary psychology, which has recently made its way into information science (Cole, 2008; Madden, 2004; Pirolli, 2007; Spink, 2010), looks at the broadest, most fundamental motivation for human information behavior and human behavior generally: our survival as a species. Survival, in turn, is dependent on humans becoming aware of changes occurring in their environment so that they can adapt to these changes. Pirolli's (2007) Information Foraging Theory, for example, categorizes humans as informavores—"a species that hungers for information in order to gather it and store it as a means for adapting to the world" (Pirolli, 2007, p. 13; for the term "informavore," see also Miller, 1983b). In order to be able to adapt, the knowledge structures, schemata, or frames humans utilize to gather, store, and structure environmental information stimuli contain what have been called "Darwinian algorithms," which are there for "organizing experience into adaptively meaningful schemes or frames" (Dubrovsky, 2002, p. 4).

The cognitive architecture of humans with this adaptive feature has been studied in evolutionary psychology by examining artifacts left by Paleolithic and Neolithic era humans. In a Paleolithic study, Donald (1991) compares the artifacts left behind by humans to the artifacts of Neanderthals. He asks the question: What separates the two species in terms of their way of thinking, their cognitive architecture? Donald hypothesizes that the key development is a change in the human knowledge structure, allowing it to encompass elements beyond episodic or experience-oriented information: As a result of this evolutionary change in cognitive architecture, humans developed a "mythic culture."

Lewis-Williams and Pearce (2005) examine the central role of mythology in Neolithic human development, based on the complicated tunnels the Neoliths built on the east coast of Ireland and elsewhere. The Ireland Neoliths built passage tombs to the dead, which were similar to but preceded Stonehenge. Lewis-Williams and Pearce contend that these tunnels duplicated an aspect of the neurological structure of the human brain evidenced when a person is in a half-sleep/half-awake state. The information need that these tunnels served—essentially the need of the living to ask the dead what is on the other side—establishes perhaps the deepest level of human information need: the need to establish our position vis-à-vis our existence as an abstract entity—our reason or purpose for being. This deep, essential level of information need was so powerful and so important, according to Lewis-Williams and Pearce's thesis (following Cauvin, 2000), that the mythological imperative preceded and led to the development of stable, stationary farming culture; not, as is commonly viewed, the other way around (Lewis-Williams and Pearce, 2005).

8.4.2.1 Toward Theory: Proposition 6

The evolutionary perspective positions information, information need, and information seeking at the center of human existence (e.g., Kaplan, 1992), as a primary element of being human, enabling humans to "process information in ways that lead to adaptive behavior" (Cosmides and Tooby, 1987, p. 282), which ensures our survival as a species. It is the thesis of Donald (1991) and Lewis-Williams and Pearce (2005) that the ultimate species-level purpose of ensuring species survival has been facilitated by the human need for information that positions humans in relation to our existential position vis-à-vis the world around us, which may be a neurologically based need.

Our sixth and last proposition in our developing theory of information need concerns information need as an adaptive mechanism.

Taylor calls information inquiry a "shifting non-linear adaptive mechanism" (Taylor, 1968, p. 179). In this chapter, we have reduced the adaptive mechanism in information need to three levels: 1) at the level of perception, for example, when a person enters a new room (Minsky, 1975); 2) at the level of humans constantly positioning ourselves in our physical and social environments (Dervin, 2003a, 2003b); and 3) at the level of the survival of the species (Donald, 1991; Lewis-Williams and Pearce, 2005). But Point 3 also includes the need for humans to position themselves at an existential level, vis-à-vis our position in the "cosmos" (as Lewis-Williams and Pearce put it), by building tunnels to the dead so we can seek information from them about what is on the other side. Lewis-Williams and Pearce's hypothesis that this existential need for information incited the Neolithic revolution and agriculture settlement, rather than the other way around, indicates the importance of this adaptive imperative as the underlying need in every human information need situation, including information search with an information system. We put this adaptive aspect of information need in a final proposition.

> **Proposition 6**: Information need is at its deepest level primarily a *human adaptive mechanism*—at the level of human perception, at the level of society and the world in which the individual operates, and at the level of survival as a species. At its deepest Q1 level, information need is an adaptive mechanism touching on 1) a survival imperative but also 2) an existential imperative (i.e., seeking meaning in the tunnel), with 2) perhaps being the conduit to imperative 1).

8.5 A Theory of Information Need

The intention of this chapter was to develop a theory of information need. From the sections interspersed throughout the chapter entitled "Toward Theory," we developed six propositions upon which the theory of information need is based:

1. We assume a *Vertical Interpretation* of Taylor's model of information need, which means that every information search to an information system consists of Taylor's four information need levels, even command-type searches

when the user is searching for an answer and knows the item or the form of the answer needed.

2. The user's information need does not evolve; only *aspects* of the topic the user selects to investigate *evolve* or shift over the course of an information search.

3. The type of information *use evolves* as the user's information seeking progresses through the *Pre-focus, Focusing, and Post-focus* stages. There is a building-up of the user's information need frame type of information use in the Pre-focus stage; a deep transformational use in the Focusing stage; and a command, known answer or known form of answer use in the Post-focus stage.

4. The theory takes an *information seeking* perspective on information search, which emphasizes an information system as a *knowledge formation/acquisition system*, thus the importance of Taylor's three Q1–Q3 question levels in this perspective.

5. Taylor's Q2–Q3 levels of information need require a *social framing* input as informational message objects (reports, tests, essays, etc.) are usually socially evaluated. As examples, Belkin's ASK IR strategy gets users to put their information need into a problem–solution format, and Cole et al.'s Compare and Contrast Essay tool requires users to put their information need into a task-oriented format.

6. At its deepest Q1 level, information need operates as a *human adaptive mechanism*: At the level of perception when entering, for example, a new room, at the level of monitoring and repositioning ourselves in a constantly shifting society and world, and at the level of our survival as a species. Included in this survival imperative, information need also operates at the level of an existential imperative (i.e., seeking meaning in the tunnel). The existential imperative may be a conduit to the survival imperative.

In Figure 8.9, we summarize the Vertical Interpretation of Taylor's information need model in a "V"-shaped diagram. Taylor's Q1–Q4 levels of information need are listed down the right-hand side of the

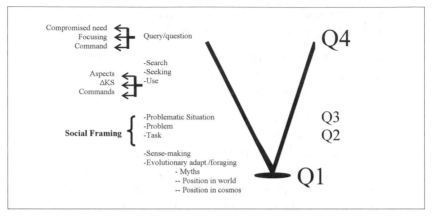

Figure 8.9 Summary of our information need analysis

"V" while the eight adjacent/surrogate concepts for information need that we discussed in the chapter are listed down the left-hand side of the "V."

In Figure 8.10, we diagram the theory of information need in a strongly visual format to facilitate the theory's utilization in information system design. The user begins a search based on an area of doubt or gap in understanding, which is a compromised form Q4 level of information need. The user with subsequent searching builds up an information need frame, borrowing generic knowledge frames from adjacent areas in memory; at a certain point, the information need actualizes in a transformational information use event, causing a focusing in information search. This transformation of information use causes the user's Q4 compromised need level to hook into the deeper Q1–Q3 levels of information need. Part of this hooking may be the user becoming aware, by being introduced to problem–goal, problem–solution, or task formulas, of the sociological aspect of the information need. We have argued in previous sections that, just as Minsky's perception frames enable people to navigate through their environment based on knowledge structures encoding past experience with an event or object (e.g., about a "room"), so too do problem and task-based frames serve as containers that facilitate the information system user becoming aware of and adapting to tried and true society-approved formulas for managing and communicating information. The user's behavior in managing the problem or performing the task is also evaluated, in large part, by organizations and institutions in the outside world, which increases the weight of this adaptive

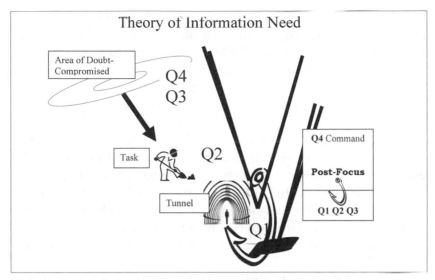

Figure 8.10   A theory of information need in visualized format

level of our information need theory. We have argued, however, that the sociological level of information need is not a full entry to the deepest Q1 level.

In Figure 8.10, at the deepest Q1 level of the theory of information need, the user metaphorically goes through a tunnel to position him- or herself in the world at both a survival level and an existential level. The tunnel aspect of the theory has particular potential in information system design because, in order to actualize the complete information need frame in the focus phase, the theory mandates strong aesthetic and experiential (i.e., affective) components. The basic assumption of the theory is that in order to be truly effective, an information system must appeal to or align with the very deepest level of the user's information need for every single user question or query. When users hook their Q4 expression of their information need in the query into the Q1 deepest level of their need, thus achieving focus (shown by the linked box on the right-hand side of the figure), the four levels of the need become extant in the search, leading to highly efficient command-type searches.

8.6 Implications of the Theory of Information Need

The theory of information need given here differentiates information need from the performance of an information-based task and the type of information searches involved in seeking and searching for information for the task. An information-based task and the types of information searches can be divided into phases. However, the information need, according to our theory, is not divided into phases. This is a difficult point that we wish to underline here.

It is commonly assumed in information science (since, in particular, Schamber, Eisenberg, and Nilan, 1990) that the user's information need evolves over the course of a task, with the user's knowledge structure constantly evolving from the beginning of the task to the end of the task as the user gathers more knowledge about the task. It seems logical to say that the information need becomes sharper, more specific. But we do not agree with this. We believe this is the wrong way to put it. The correct way to put it is that the information need manifests itself to the user in a more specific way as the user nears task completion.

There is a difference between saying that 1) the user's information need evolves over the course of performing an information-based task and 2) the user's information need manifests itself differently over the course of performing a task.

The theory of information need proposed here divides the performance of an information-based task (e.g., doing a project, solving a problem, completing an assignment) into Pre-focus, Focusing, and Post-focus. There is one information need instantiation, in the Focusing stage. The information need, once it instantiates to its deepest Q1 level, then stays the same. In the Post-focus stage of performing the task, therefore, the information need stays the same as the user conducts command-type information searches (Known item or Known form of answer searches).

It is perhaps the Pre-focus stage of performing an information-based task that is the source of confusion. The user's information need appears to evolve because the user is constantly shifting the query. But the theory of information need we propose denies that the user's information need is evolving. Rather, the user's investigation of aspects of the topic evolves in the Pre-focus stage. There is a background and a foreground to information need. The evolving investigation of topic aspects in the Pre-focus stage of performing a task is the background. The information need emerges from the background to form the foreground in the Focusing Stage. We will illustrate this difficult underlying idea of our theory in Part II of this book.

Part **II**

Information Need in Pre-Focus and Focusing Stages and How It Works

CHAPTER 9

How Information Need Works

In Part I we proposed a theory of information need based on six propositions. The theory determined that there are three types of information search that occur in the three phases of performing any information-dependent task/project/assignment, etc.:

1. Pre-focus: The user investigates a shifting series of aspects of the broad topic of the search. There is a problem of information overload in the results list.

2. Focusing: The user instantiates the information need frame to the deepest Q1 level.

3. Post-focus: The user makes known item or known form of answer-oriented commands to the information system to obtain evidentiary or support information for idea or focus statement, argument, or thesis.

The information need manifests itself to the user differently in the Pre-focus, Focusing, and Post-focus phases of performing an information-based task, but the theory claims that the information need of the user does not in fact evolve over the different phases of the user performing the task or researching and writing a project. Before the focus, the user's information need is not yet there; it has not yet instantiated. And after focus has occurred, when the user is in the Post-focus stage of performing the task, the information need remains the same (unless the user aborts the need because of a superior's dissatisfaction with it or for some other reason). In the Post-focus stage, the theory's conceptualization of information need and information search as a command based human activity reconciles the information science perspective on need with that of computer science. The dialectic between the two perspectives and the objective to take each into account is a primary goal of the theory of information need we propose in this book.

The theory takes this nontraditional approach to information need because its fundamental proposition is that, in order to really become intuitive for most of us and to be useful to the disadvantaged in our society who now do not use information to its full advantage, information systems must become attached to knowledge formation. Only through knowledge formation can the disadvantaged become involved in the information age and exercise their information needs through information use during the information access activity of information search.

In Part II, we look at how information need works when the user is in the Pre-focus and Focusing stages of performing a task/project/ assignment, etc. that requires the user to conduct information searches. For both the user in a Pre-focus stage and a user in the Focusing stage, we elaborate and further explain the theory by using supporting evidence, primarily from Cole's (1994a) study of PhD history students' information processes while researching and writing their dissertation. Part II ends with corroborating evidence from subsequent studies.

CHAPTER 10

The User's Situation
in the Pre-Focus Search

We open Part II by reviewing the situation of the user in a Pre-focus stage of performing an information-based task who is perusing the results list. What is this person going through? How can we characterize his or her information need? And how does the information need work when the Pre-focus user is performing an information-based task?

We briefly backtrack. In Part I, we operationalized the user's information need as two contrasting conceptions: 1) the computer science perspective on the user's information need during information search, and 2) the information science perspective on the user's information need during information search. The computer science position is that the user has a strong conceptualization of the information need throughout the search, therefore the user is commanding the information system for an answer. The information science position on the user's information need is completely different. This position has the user constantly shifting or evolving the investigation of the aspects of the general topic, all along the time interval of the information search, especially while perusing the results list. The information science position defines the user's information need as weakly conceptualized, so weakly conceptualized that the user loses sight of it during the search session. Information from the system changes what the user thinks he or she "needs" to investigate, and he or she becomes interested in investigating these other aspects of the general topic.

In Figure 10.1 we diagram these two conceptions of the user's information need during information search while the user is perusing the results list. On the left-hand side of the figure, labeled "A," is the computer science position. The user has a strong conception of the information need and maintains the same information need

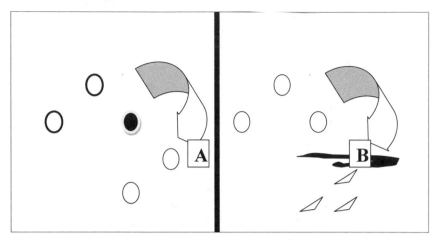

Figure 10.1 Two concepts of information need's shift in perspective during a single information search session

throughout the search session, even while perusing the results list. Any change the user makes in expanding or revising the initial query is a result of feedback gleaned from information found in the results list and elsewhere that enables the user to correct the alignment.

On the right-hand side of Figure 10.1, labeled "B," the information science position on the user's information need while perusing the results list is completely different. Here, the user has a weak conception of the information need and the need is not *manifested* to the user the same throughout the search session, especially while perusing the results list. The aspects of the search topic the user wishes to investigate are shifted or made to evolve as a result of the information the user discovers about the topic in the results list. (See Figure 11.1 for links to "A" and "B.")

We have conceptualized Figure 10.1 and these two different A and B perspectives in terms of Minsky's (1975) frame theory. The information science position on the user is analogous to a person who perceptually/cognitively interacts with his or her environment without a map; it is like this person is taking discrete snapshots of the environment through which he or she is traversing, but with no strong frame or map to link the discrete snapshots together. It is like a person traveling through a strange city without a map, or without a firm conception of the city or where he or she is going and how to get there. There is no meaning to the passing buildings, streets, and passersby. They all look disconnected.

The computer science position on the user, on the other hand, presumes that the user perceptually/cognitively interacts with the environment using a map—a dominating information need frame. The map or frame is able to link together the discrete snapshots of the environment through which he or she is traversing; the snapshots now can be seen as having an order and a meaning. The passing landmark buildings on the map indicate this user is getting closer to the destination. The clothes of the passersby take on significance because they indicate this person is getting closer to the entertainment district or the business district, which is also signified on the user's map or frame. All the buildings, streets, and passersby look connected with the meaning given to the person's purpose by the strong information need frame.

For the information science position on the user, conducting an information search during the Pre-focus or exploratory phase of performing a task/project/assignment is difficult for everyone because they do not yet have the strong frame of reference for their information need that a focus brings to information search. Without a strong frame of reference providing criteria for judging relevance, the Pre-focus stage makes it difficult to utilize the results list because everything looks the same—there is no touchstone for making relevance judgments and deciding which of the citations in the results list best aligns with the initial information need or query.

In addition, the Pre-focus stage provides a huge barrier to, in particular, the disadvantaged in society because it takes a certain amount of skill and experience to construct a strong conceptualization of information need during the information search. In the theory of information need given in Part I, Chapter 8, the user's task gives a great deal of information to the user about his or her information need. The disadvantaged often don't have these information-based skills. Also, to effectively get through the Pre-focus stage to a focus, one must be able to construct a focus (theme, argument, thesis point of view) from, at first, seemingly disparate pieces of information. It is the phase that turns off a huge proportion of the population, causing high dropout rates in school; and for those who complete school, it is the source of lack of original work or effective work when their information-based task requires critical thinking. Critical thinking only evolves as a result of constructing a focus, which takes a certain amount of Pre-focus information gathering, thinking, and so on. Original work requires slogging through information overload, reading without a focus. As a result, it is difficult to ascribe purpose and meaning to this Pre-focus information search task.

This Pre-focus reading, where the user must try to absorb information while conducting an information search, is in a certain sense difficult because it requires the user to determine an overview of the topic, its issues, problems, and so on, from the chaotic information provided in the results list. The slow gathering and putting together of the topic's structure is an essential part of creating and building a threshold from which original, critical thinking can emerge. It is the work for work's sake part of the formation of an idea or a perspective on the task the person is doing. But it must be done. If we understand what happens to the user's information need when the user is in a Pre-focus stage of performing a task, solving a problem, and so on, while he or she is perusing the results list, information scientists can build information systems that assist these users to traverse the information overload barrier.

10.1 Pre-Focus Search: Operational Definition

In this section, we provide an operational definition for the user in a Pre-focus stage of performing an information-based task. As you will see, the definition is centered on the concept of selection, which is a traditional, age-old information science concept. Finally, we will illustrate how selection works during Pre-focus searching.

As stated in Part I, the traditional computer science model of the user and the user's information need when interacting with an information system is a command or answer-based need. This is in contrast to the information science model, which is based on the user exploring the information system for information that will provide information for ill-defined questions; this latter model of the information user during information search renders the user's query a much less efficient representation of a much more complex user information need.

Our conceptualization of information need, and the theory of it proposed in Part I, requires various kinds of information search. In this section, we *operationalize* the distinction in terms of type of information search rather than type of information need. The traditional, computer science model of the user is wholly directed to a narrow spectrum of information searches, while the information science model of information need is directed to a much wider spectrum of searches. The information need theory in Part I allows for the computer science conception of type of information search in the Post-focus phase of the user seeking information for a task/problem/assignment and so forth.

We differentiated the computer science and information science perspectives on information need as command or answer seeking for computer science and question or information seeking for information science. In terms of information search type, the traditional, computer science conception of information search is what is referred to in information science as a known item or known answer (or known form of answer) search. Known item search is the basic, default-type search upon which the classic library tools such as catalogs, indexes and abstracts were built. Subsequent studies have shown this to be the predominant search type. Library catalog studies done in the 1960s at Yale University, the University of Michigan, and the Ann Arbor Public Library determined that between 65 and 80 percent of all searches were for known items (Lipetz, 1970, p. 7). However, both known item and unknown item types of searches have a long tradition in information science, which we will briefly describe here (for a longer treatment, see Cole, Julien, and Leide, 2010).

We divide searching into known item and unknown item searching; the latter term includes subject/topic and exploratory browsing searching (University of California Libraries, Bibliographic Services Task Force, 2005; Wildemuth and O'Neill, 1995). Other terms frequently used to denote searching types are purposive, semipurposive, and undirected searching (Bawden, 1986). The dichotomous term for known item search, 'unknown item search,' is rarely used in today's search-type taxonomies (Lee, Renear, and Smith, 2006), even when known item search is included in the taxonomy (e.g., Meadow, Boyce, Kraft, and Barry, 2007, p. 278). However, there are no hard and fast categories of types of information search. In Figure 10.2, we diagram all types of information searches in the earlier statement on a known to unknown item continuum, starting from a known item search where the user has complete and accurate information about the known item, located at the far left-hand side of the figure, and ending with an unknown item, full-on exploratory search, located at the far right-hand side of the figure. While the discussion that follows focuses on four distinct points on the continuum, the continuum is meant to include all types of searches, including those we do not discuss here.

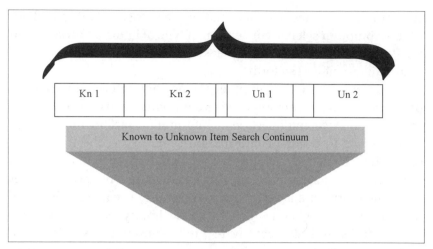

Figure 10.2 Known (Kn 1 and Kn 2) to unknown (Un 1 and Un 2) item search continuum

Searching for a known item and searching for an unknown item are two entirely different activities, involving different user cognitive processes, but it is necessary to nuance this statement.

In Known Item Search 1, the user has complete and accurate information about the known item, giving this user maximum certainty going into the search of the index or catalog. For this search, the primary purpose of the index or catalog is to show the user whether the library owns the known item and, if so, where, via the classification code, the item can be physically located; either in the library where the user is at that moment (Lancaster and Joncich, 1977, p. 19), or in some other location via interlibrary loan (Svenonius, 2000). By typing in all the attributes of the known item in the query, the system, in theory, produces a one-item-long results list, from which the user can immediately write down the item location code. If the item is not in the database, the results list will be empty. (We make the assumption that the index or cataloging record contains no mistakes and that the IR system does not provide approximate citations to the user in the results list.) This search can be termed a Perfect Match Search.

In Known Item Search 2, the user has a state of mind based on the knowledge or belief that the sought-for item exists (Lee, Renear, and Smith, 2006), but the user has incomplete or inaccurate information about the known item (for an example of this type of search, see Matthews, Lawrence, Ferguson, and Council on Library Resources,

1983, p. 90; see also Dwyer, Gossen, and Martin, 1991; Lewis, 1987; Swanson, 1972). Uncertainty occurs in the user the moment the IR system responds to the incomplete or inaccurate information by producing a set of alternative items that it deems to be approximate to the user's input of information about the known item. The user must then identify the sought-for item from this set of like items by looking at the item's characteristics on the catalog or index record. The assemblage "enable[s] a user to identify a document uniquely and thus distinguish [it] from similar ones" (Borgman, 2000, p. 74). When the user has incomplete or inaccurate information about the known item, the index or catalog record is particularly designed for facilitating the matching process between the user's mental image of the known item and the record of the item in the index or catalog. The index or catalog record assembles not only all the necessary identification attributes or dimensions of the item in a formulaic fashion, but it often does this in a more complete and more accurate manner than in the actual physical item by getting this information from external sources. The user quickly identifies gaps and inaccuracies about the known item. This search can be termed a Best Match Search, meaning the user must identify and select the record that best (not perfectly) matches his or her original inaccurate or incomplete mental image of the known item. Known Item Search 2, where the user has incomplete or inaccurate information about the known item, is extremely common.

In Unknown Item Search 1, the user knows how to describe what he or she is looking for, therefore enabling this user to formulate a precise and efficient query, the traditional start state for utilizing the index or catalog. An example of this type of search is: Who is the governor of Alaska? There is a precise answer for this type of search, the general parameters of which the user has in mind before the search. It has even been argued that this type of subject/topic search is in fact a form of known item search. According to Bates (1998, p. 1186), "knowledge specifically of what is wanted [leads to] a 'known-item' search." Again, as there will be more than one item in the results list, this is a best match (not perfect match) type of search.

In Unknown Item Search 2, and contrary to the previous three search types, users only know "fringes of a gap in [their] knowledge," making it extremely difficult for them to identify and describe the information gap or need (Bates, 1998, p. 1186). Because these users do not have knowledge of their information need when the search commences (Belkin, Oddy, and Brooks, 1982a; Borgman, 2000), they cannot identify an effective start state from which to form a query and to utilize the catalog effectively. Of all the four searches described in Figure 10.2, the user in Unknown Item Search 2 has a mental image of the search that is, in fact, in an "asymmetrical" relationship with the catalog or index (Bates, 1998, p. 1186). This is also a best match type of search, producing a results list that is long and especially difficult for the user to understand or process, but this is an extreme example of best match. It is not really what the user in this search situation requires, which is information pertaining to the "question-type" information need. In Part I, we have defined this activity of the user as "aspect" investigation or "aspect matching"—the user matching his or her mental representation of the developing information need with the information received from the results list.

We operationalize the computer science model of information search with Known Item Search 1 and 2, and Unknown Item Search 1. We operationalize the information science model of information search when the user is in a Pre-focus phase of performing a task, solving a problem, and so on with Unknown Item Search 2. By doing so, we introduce the concepts of the perfect match system, the best match system, and the aspect matching system, which we attach, respectively, to (a) Known Item Search 1, Known Item Search 2, and Unknown Item Search 1, and (b) Unknown Item Search 2. We diagram this distinction in Figure 10.3.

Figure 10.3 outlines in black-and-white terms the difference between the computer science and information science position on the user's mental image of what the user expects to see in the information system results list before commencing the information search. The aspect matching of a user conducting Unknown Item Search 2 is the subject of the chapters that follow.

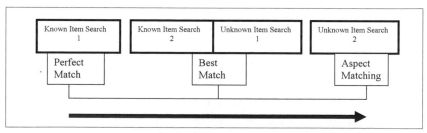

Figure 10.3   Known Item and Unknown Item Search types and Perfect and Best Match, plus Aspect Matching

CHAPTER 11

The Situation of User's Information Need in Pre-Focus Information Search

We now diagram in Figure 11.1 the situation of the user's information need when the user is in Pre-focus information search while this user is perusing the results list. We have previously operationalized the types of searches, reducing them to four discrete points on a continuum of searches:

- Known Item Search 1

- Known Item Search 2

- Unknown Item Search 1

- Unknown Item Search 2

We defined the computer science conception of the user's information need as Known Item Search 1 (perfect match), but with allowance for Known Item Search 2 and Unknown Item Search 1 (best match). These latter two types of searches are posited on the notion that the user has a strong conception of the information need because they are making a command to the information system for an answer they have a strong mental model about. The information science conception, on the other hand, we defined as Unknown Item Search 2. This is the information situation of the user conducting a Pre-focus information search while perusing the results list.

In Figure 11.1 we diagram these two positions on the user's information need. In "A," at the top of the figure, we diagram the computer science position on the user's information need while perusing the results list, indicating it applies to Known Item Search 1 and 2, and Unknown Item Search 1. In "B," at the bottom of the figure, we diagram the information science position on the user's information need while the user is conducting a Pre-focus search and is perusing the results list, indicating it applies to Unknown Item Search 2.

A. For the computer science command or answer-oriented perspective on the user's information need while perusing the results list, the user maintains a firm hold on the initiating information need utilized to formulate the initial query to the information system. The results list is easy to utilize because the user has a firm grasp of the relative relevance of the citations in the list, and can easily spot the most relevant citation for the need—i.e., it contains the answer he or she is seeking when utilizing the information system. There are Noise considerations

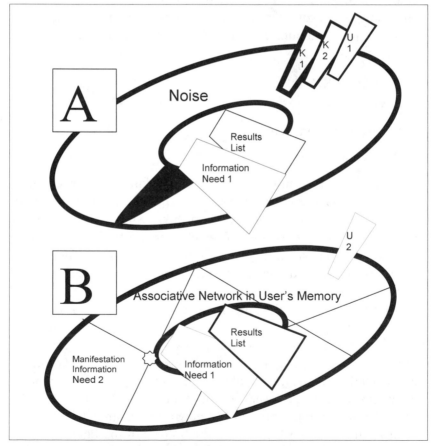

Figure 11.1 The associative network for A) Known Item Search 1 and 2, and Unknown Item Search 1 versus B) Unknown Item Search 2

produced by false drops, among other factors, in the
results list. For Known Item Search 2, where the user has
inaccurate or incomplete information about the known
item, there is also a form of Noise.

B. For the information science question-oriented
perspective on the Pre-focus user's information need
while perusing the results list, the user does not maintain
a firm hold on the initiating information need utilized to
formulate the initial query to the information system. The
information need for Unknown Item Search 2, where the
user is in a Pre-focus, exploratory stage, is not strong
enough to provide strong relevance criteria. The user,
because he or she is operating in Association Wheel
mode, finds his or her attention wandering from the
original aspects being investigated, from which the
original query to the system was formed. As a result of
what is seen in the results list, the user now wishes to
investigate other aspects that come to mind.

In Figure 11.1 "B," we refer to the Association Wheel, which sym-
bolically represents the user's associative network stored in memory.
In a Pre-focus stage information search when the user is perusing the
results list, the user's initial information need formulation in the
query is dominated by information elements in the results list, which
cause the user to associate with them different elements in memory.
The Association Wheel represents networked memory. The associated element in memory will "select" the aspect the user will pursue
next. The Association Wheel and the selection concept are described
in the following chapters.

CHAPTER 12

The Selection Concept

We have operationalized the computer science model and the information science model of the user's information need via two different kinds of information searches: the Known Item Search and the Unknown Item Search, each of which has two subtypes. In the previous section, we associated Known Item Search 1 and 2 and Unknown Item Search 1 with the computer science perspective on information need; we associated Unknown Item Search 2 with the information science perspective on information need when the user is in a Pre-focus phase of performing a task, solving a problem, and so on. To further describe the underlying concepts that occur when the user peruses the results list when in a Pre-focus, exploratory phase of performing an information-dependent task, we discuss here the concept of selection.

There are two key sources of definitions for the selection concept in information science: Cutter's three objectives for a dictionary catalog and Vannevar Bush's selection concept for a hypertext-based information system called the memex (for further discussion, see Cole, Julien, and Leide, 2010).

12.1 Cutter's Selection Concept in Traditional Indexing and Cataloging

We begin our discussion of the selection concept by defining how it has been used in traditional indexing and cataloging as the concept was seminally articulated in Cutter's (1904, p. 12) three objectives for a dictionary catalog:

1. To enable a person to find a book of which the author, title, or the subject is known

2. To show what a library has by a given author, on a given subject, or in a given kind of literature (poetry, drama, fiction)

3. To assist in the choice of a work as to its edition (bibliographical), or as to its character (literary or topical)

The Cutter objectives have been commonly interpreted as, respectively:

1. The finding objective (for a book of which the author, title, or subject is known)

2. The identifying objective (via collocation or bringing together like items in one place in the catalog)

3. The selection objective (from among items previously identified as pertinent) (Svenonius, 2000, pp. 14–15; for the re-interpretation of Cutter's objectives over the years, see Svenonius, 2000)

Two caveats must be given before beginning our analysis:

A. The three objectives are concerned with facilitating or supporting user information search as a second-order goal, their first-order goal being the creation of an effective catalog, to be evaluated by how well the catalog itself performs or serves its intended purpose (for a discussion of this point, see Lee, Renear, and Smith, 2006). Here, we shift the discussion of the objectives from catalog performance to the broader perspective of the information search.

B. Also, we interpret the first objective narrowly, as a finding objective for an item that is known to the user (Baker and Lancaster, 1991, p. 200).

Our slant on Cutter's objectives enables us to interpret them to mean that they operate together for certain kinds of searches, but for other types of searches they either work together less or not at all. From this point of view, the first (finding) objective appears to be straightforward. The user has information about a particular item and wants to see if the item exists in the collection and, if so, from where, via the location code, it can be obtained. Most users search for a known item via the item's title; a search for a known item via the subject is less efficient (Baker and Lancaster, 1991, p. 274). Searching for a known item via its subject heading is unusual and inefficient because the search then becomes like a keyword search, which leads to many citations in the results list the user must go through to find the known item (Lee, Renear, and Smith, 2006). It is far simpler when searching for a known item to put the exact title words in the search box, which, in theory, produces a results list with very few items in it (showing different editions of the same item, etc.). An advanced search where all information about the known item can be input into the information system by the user, in theory, reduces the results list to one item, the item being sought by the user. The user then obtains the location number for the known item and retrieves it from its physical location in the library or information center.

The second (identification) and third (selection) objectives, on the other hand, are dealing with greater user uncertainty and involve deeper cognitive operations on the part of the user. For example, the second identification objective, when it is implemented in a catalog, is intended to bring like items together in one place to facilitate the user finding the needed item, but it requires the user to make comparisons not only between records for items that are quite similar, so the user can pick out just the element that makes one item better than the others, but it also requires the user to manage and supervise this matching process via a detailed mental image of the needed item in working memory.

Based on the search definitions in the previous section, we make the following statements comparing the perfect match Known Item Search 1 with the best match Known Item Search 2 and aspect match Unknown Item Search 2:

- Known Item Search 1 is, in theory, totally focused toward Cutter's first finding objective, while best match Known Item Search 2 brings into play Cutter's third selection objective.

- Therefore, the role of Cutter's second identification objective is greater for Known Item Search 2 than for Known Item Search 1.

- And even greater for Unknown Item Search 2.

We illustrate these three statements in Figure 12.1, where Cutter's identification second objective is shown as a sliding scale between Cutter's finding first objective and Cutter's selection third objective. The identifying scale exerts more power for aspect match Unknown

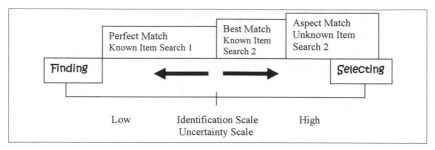

Figure 12.1   An illustration of the dynamic scales of Cutter's three objectives for the perfect match Known Item Search 1 versus the best match Known Item Search 2 and the aspect match Unknown Item Search 2

Item Search 2 and for best match Known Item Search 2, and much less power the closer the search is to the theoretical notion of a perfect match Known Item Search 1. We also associate the user's uncertainty with the identifying scale—the higher the user uncertainty about the search, the greater the utilization of the identifying scale.

The point we raise here is the importance of the concepts of selection and identification for the information science perspective on the user's information need while he or she is trying to decipher the results list. Selecting and identifying come into play for all searches, except for Known Item Search 1—and only then for the ideal case where the results list contains only the sought for item, indicating a perfect match between the user's query and the results list.

12.2 Vannevar Bush's Selection Concept

For his associative indexing concept, Bush incorporated the associationism concepts introduced in Chapter 11. He envisaged a new form of indexing: a more human, natural way. "[The human mind] operates by association," he wrote. "With one item in its grasp, it snaps instantly to the next [item] that is suggested by the association of thoughts ... " (Bush, 1945, p. 106). The central concept of the memex's associative indexing system is selection:

> [The memex] affords an immediate step, however, to associative indexing, the basic idea of which is the provision whereby any item may be caused at will to *select* immediately and automatically another. This is the essential feature of the memex. (Bush, 1945, p. 107, emphasis added)

Bush operationalizes his concept of selection when he describes the procedure of selection for a fingerprint-matching machine:

> This process is simple *selection*: it proceeds by examining in turn every one of a large *set of items*, and by *picking out* those which have certain specified characteristics. (Bush, 1945, p. 106, emphasis added)

Bush's term "picking out" can mean three different things according to the *Oxford Dictionary of Current English* (1984, p. 554):

A. *Taking*, which denotes the physical part of selection when the user *obtains* the needed item. In IR, obtaining occurs when the user either clicks on a hyperlink or by some other method (i.e., by typing in a new URL, by taking the item from the shelf, obtaining the item from another library via ILL, etc.).

B. *Identifying or recognizing*, which denotes an earlier phase of selection than A, where the person first must identify or recognize an item.

C. *Distinguishing*, which denotes a further refinement or phase to the user's process of identifying or recognizing a needed item (i.e., the user identifies or recognizes the needed item by distinguishing the needed item from surrounding objects in the set).

With these dictionary definitions, we can refine Bush's two-step process (from his previous quote), giving us the following, elaborated definition of his concept of selection:

1. The user first examines a set of items,

2. "Identifying or recognizing" from the set those with "certain specified characteristics," via the act of

A. "Distinguishing" the needed item from the surrounding objects in the set. Distinguishing therefore implies the act of eliminating unusable or unwarranted associations from consideration (see the associative memory theory discussion in subsequent chapters).

3. Finally, the user takes or obtains the selected item (off the library shelf or by some other physical act like clicking on a hyperlinked citation).

We examine this elaborated definition of Bush's concept of selection in more detail in the next section.

We further specify the identification concept 2.A in our definition by briefly situating Bush's memex machine in the context of the overall development of an information retrieval machine that culminated in the memex, called the rapid selector machine. The rapid selector machine was first conceptualized in Germany in 1927 by Emanuel Goldberg before development shifted to the U.S. in the 1938–1940 prewar period with a team led by Bush (Buckland, 1992). The rapid selector was in response to the explosion of data of all kinds and the inability of traditional, hierarchically based cataloging and indexing systems to handle these new, information retrieval tasks (Burke, 1992). Bush, for example, proposed building the rapid selector for the FBI to facilitate fingerprint matching (Burke and Buckland, 1994).

The rapid selector machine worked on the principle of a quick and accurate information retrieval of a required microfilm document via a coding system, referred to as 'the associations,' each of which represented an important element of the document. The associations were punched into a stationary card in prescribed positions. When the user inserted the stationary coded card into the selector machine, it was then matched to all documents in the database via the coded associations. "A perfect match between the codes on [the microfilm document abstract frame] and the codes on [the stationary] card triggered the selection circuit" (Burke, 1992, pp. 150–151). Buckland (1992, p. 286) refers to the matching as "the coincidence of a pattern on the microfilm matching the pattern on the search card." Because this was a perfect match IR system, each of the association codes took on enormous importance. In effect, each "[important/elemental] datum had its own identity" (Otlet, 1934, quoted in Buckland, 1992, p. 290).

The key point that each association code in the rapid selector's matching process had its own identity allows us to further specify our development of Bush's selection concept, to the following form:

1. The user first examines a set of items,

2. "Identifying or recognizing" from the set those with "certain specified characteristics," via the act of

A. Giving identity to specified characteristics, distinguishing the needed item, via these specified characteristics, from the surrounding objects in the set, which involves:

    I. Keeping the items in the set that have the specified characteristics.

    II. Weeding out unusable and unwarranted associations from consideration.

3. The user takes or obtains the selected item by some physical action.

We extensively reference this detailed definition of the selection concept in the next sections. The selection concept is one of the most powerful conceptualizations in information. Its greatest strength is that it allows insight into human reasoning, how we think, and the role of information need and information in these processes.

12.3 How Selection Works in Pre-Focus Search

To describe how the selection concept works in a Pre-focus information search, we bring back Part I's division of the user's perceptual/cognitive information system, which we defined as five circles (see Chapter 7 in Part I). We reproduce the five circles diagram here for easy reference in Figure 12.2.

The circles indicate an induction or bottom-up perspective on perceptual processing, suited to defining, following MacKay, information need as a concept geared to enable human adaptation to changes in the environment, which can be both physical and social environments. Information need commences from the environment, an unfamiliar stimulus sent to the human organism that defies the expectation state of that organism. Similarly, the bottom-up perspective on perception that follows is primarily based on Harnad's (1987a, b) inductive or bottom-up view of human reasoning whereby unfamiliar stimuli from the environment, once received by the human sensory system, are processed first into categories before top down knowledge systems come into play in labeling the categories as concepts (for the opposite hypothesis that all categories are innate, see Chomsky, 1980; Fodor, 1985).

The start of an information need in this book is assumed to be bottom-up. That is, an information need is part of the evolutionary development of humans and its principle utility is to enable humans to recognize changes in the environment and adapt to them and thus survive as a species (see in information science, Berul, 1969; in cognitive psychology, Harnad, 1987a, b). This is a fundamental conceptualization of information need to which we refer in much greater detail in subsequent chapters.

What follows is based on the categorical perception (CP) theory of Harnad (1987a). Harnad gives a full explanation of human processing of environmental stimulus information beginning as a bottom-up process. He postulates that we first process a stimulus into a category; we categorize the stimulus in terms of our past experience with the object, event, or even, when reading text, "an abstract idea such as goodness or truth" (Harnad, 1987b, p. 1). Categorization is, in effect, a perceptual-cum-cognitive "sorting activity" (Harnad, 1987b, p. 1). There are stimuli that are easy to categorize and stimuli that are difficult to categorize, a distinction that is determined by the amount of top-down processing that occurs in the particular categorizing instance. This basically means that the more experience the individual has with the stimulus being categorized, the more top-down processing occurs. If there is no experience with the stimulus, then bottom-up processes more heavily come into play. The bottom-up instance relies heavily on sensory, motor, and neural systems for the categorization, but does eventually involve the top-down cognitive memory functions (Harnad, 1987b). There is a contradiction seen in some of the literature concerning this point.

Decoding (by categorizing) and identifying the category (labeling the category with a concept term), as a result of inserting the category into an individual's symbolic system, allows symbolic response in thinking, speaking, or writing activities, or, in the case that concerns us here, in information activities.

We will divide this chapter on how selection works in Pre-focus search into Circles 1–2 and Circles 2–3, with particular emphasis on Circle 2 and Circle 3. The main concentration of what follows is Circle 2, indicated in Figure 12.2 by two converging arrows. After the human organism receives stimulus information from the environment, it must first sort the signal into categories. Categorization occurs in Circle 2. However, conceptualization of the environmental stimulus also begins in Circle 2: thus, the meeting here of the perceptual and cognitive systems. Generally speaking, perception is the act of categorization whereas cognition is the conceptualization of that category by inserting it in a symbolic, concept-based system. These two

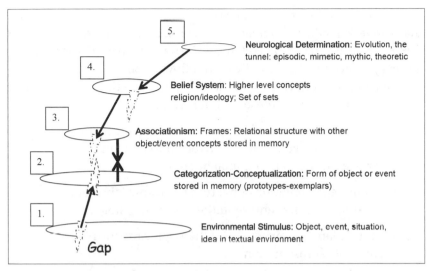

Figure 12.2 Environmental stimulus (Circle 1) leading to Gap, categorization (Circle 2), leading to Knowledge structure formation in cases where no knowledge structure exists

systems, the perceptual and cognitive system, utilize different coding schemes for the transmission of signals from the environment. In Harnad's (1987a) words, it is where the analog signal from the environment, detected by the sensory system of the individual, is converted, via an analog-to-digital conversion, into a discrete and labeled digital signal that can be transmitted, received, understood, and acted upon by the individual's top-down, knowledge-based conceptual processing system.

12.3.1 Circle 1 to Circle 2

We define Circles 1–2 as environmental stimulus to categorization, which is a largely perceptual process, but with cognitive or higher level knowledge input as well. However, there is a question of how user knowledge and decision processes come into play. In speech recognition, for example: How does the speech-recognizer get from the sensory data to the symbolic description stage? It must involve top-down information and knowledge formation processes. And where does that knowledge come from? (See Harnad, 1987b, p. 12.)

We want to describe the process clearly here, with the proviso that there are still many questions that remain open (Harnad, 1987a, b).

For example, as shown later in Figure 12.4, we envisage the possibility that Circle 2 could be divided into two separate circles, perhaps a Circle 2(a) and Circle 2(b). Following Harnad's (1987a) theory of categorical perception (CP), we divide the flow of environmental stimulus information from Circle 1 to Circle 2, and even through Circle 2 in Figure 12.4, into three representational systems:

1. Environmental stimulus, which is an object, event, situation, or even an idea converted to an iconic representation (i.e., a retinal image)

2. Iconic representation converted to atomic labels for invariant feature representation (parts of category)

3. Atomic labels converted into the beginning form of concept representation

Let us take the example of spatial relationships in the environment. The environmental stimulus is the analog message caught by "feature detectors" in the individual's sensory system, and these must somehow be transduced to the mind's coding scheme into some sort of symbolic form, or the language or code of thought. One theory is that the language of thought is in propositional code (Bialystok and Olson, 1987). According to Harnad:

> One of the prominent features of any propositional code is that it must operate on discrete symbols. Hence, in (say) vision, a physical object is viewed, it makes an analog projection on the retina, and then, at some stage in processing, that analog information must somehow be filtered, digitized, and turned into symbols for the propositional system to be able to operate on. (Harnad, 1987b, p. 21)

This process begins with the detection and labeling invariant features with atomic labels; let us say these could be propositional statements, like: Line A is straight. The Line A is "above" or "below" Line B. Bialystok and Olson (1987) advocate such a propositional theory. Spatial relations such as "above" and "below" are innate, and thus, according to Bialystok and Olson, "categorical." (Harnad, 1987b, p. 21). The final and third part of this part of perceptual categorization is where the Line A and its relationship to Line B enter the symbolic representational system, or "the language of thought" (Harnad, 1987b, p. 22).

We define Circle 1 to Circle 2 specifically as these three representational systems, ending in the user labeling the categorized stimulus with a concept term. Categorization is traditionally seen as a perceptual function (Bruner, 1957), where information received from the environment is in analog or sensory form. Higher order, abstract categories are constituted from these basic lower order categories. This means, for what concerns us here, that we spend more time with the third representational system. Concept labeling is the language of thinking and symbolic representation into which a user of an information system inserts a signal/message received from an information system, specifically signal/messages received as a result of perusing the system output to the user's query in the results list.

Throughout this book we have utilized Shannon's model of communication (information) flow over a channel, from the sender to the receiver. In Figure 12.3, we insert the Shannon channel in between two circles from the five-circle diagram of information flow. The point of the Shannon channel is the two transducers, one at the sender's end and the other at the receiver's end. This is because Shannon was concerned with the transmission of signals where analog messages at the sender's end had first to be converted by the transducer into a compressed signal, or into digital form. During transmission, Harnad underlines that "information is always lost" (Harnad, 1987a, p. 542), which in Shannon's channel model is "noise." This is the concern with all information or communication transmission systems today. For example, in the transmission of a television show as a real

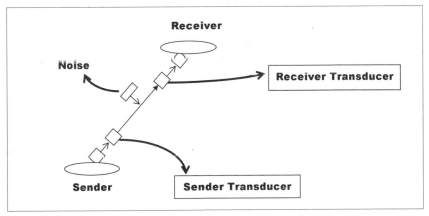

Figure 12.3 Shannon's channel of communication (information) flow over a channel from sender to receiver

performance, the analog image must be converted to digital form for transmission to receivers in homes throughout the nation. At the receiver end, the signal has to be decompressed by the receiver's transducer back into the original message, the image of the live performance. Information that drops out during the signal transmission due to noise is built into the expectation in the receiver's transducer's algorithm, allowing for fill-in of the missing information in the reconstituted message handed to the receiver by its transducer.

According to Harnad's CP theory, as an environmental stimulus makes its way up through the previously mentioned three representational systems, there are four conversion stages:

- Stage 1: O/I [object to icon conversion]

- Stage 2: I/C [icon to atomic category conversion]

- Stage 3: C/S [categorical to symbolic conversion]

- Stage 4: S/S [symbolic to symbolic conversion, or verbal to verbal conversion] (Harnad, 1987a, p. 543)

The first three stages involve analog-to-digital conversion characteristics, while the fourth stage involves strictly digital-to-digital (or refinement of the digital state arrived at in Stage 3). We will look at each of these conversions in this section, except Stage 4 S/S [symbolic to symbolic conversion], which we examine in the next section as it concerns Circle 3.

To begin, in Figure 12.4 we diagram the flow of a signal or message from the environment to the third representational system: conceptual labeling, the language of thought. The bottom circle (Circle 1) is the stimulus from the environment that starts the information need. It is heard in the hearing sensory system of the individual if it is sound or it is seen by the visual system if it is in a textual landscape such as a book, article, an internet page, and so on, which is the concern of this book.

The first representation and second representation systems of the "categorizer," which work on "two kinds of representation of the stimulus object" (or event or situation), both activate upon receiving the stimulus signal from the environment into the sensory system (Harnad, 1987a, p. 551). The first representation is iconic and in analog form: i.e., it exists as "the proximal projection of the distal stimulus object on the [sensory system's] transducer surfaces" (Harnad, 1987a, p. 551). The second representation is the categorical representation (which may either begin to form upon receiving the stimulus signal or already be formed, which means it can be matched to the stimulus). The second representation is "context sensitive," which Harnad operationalizes as the set of "relevant and confusable alternative categories" (Harnad, 1987a, p. 552). The categorical representation eliminates from the iconic representation much of the raw information, to retain only the invariant features of the stimulus. However, the categorical representation is not yet in digital or symbolic form, but remains in an analog state, or at least it is "not yet fully 'digitized'" (Harnad, 1987a, p. 552). The first iconic representation performs the *discrimination* function of the process; the second categorical representation performs the *identification* function of the process (i.e., identifying the invariants of the category). The *symbolic* representation function then occurs. The symbolic system "assigns category membership" by labeling the category "from existing labels" in the system (Harnad, 1987a, p. 554), a top-down process that creates an "encoded mental sentence" (Harnad, 1987a, p. 556).

According to Harnad's CP theory, top-down activity from what we have described as Circles 3–5 occurs immediately or almost immediately with the development of the iconic representation, which is bottom-up (provoked by the environmental stimulus object). This mixing occurs, we hypothesize, in Circle 2.

Circle 2 is therefore the crucial channel linking perception and cognition, where perceptual information from the environment is transduced (to use Shannon's term) or converted (to use Harnad's term) for transmission to the user's cognitive or symbolic system. The two systems have different coding schemes. The sensory detectors welcoming the environmental signal to the perceptual system is akin to an analog coding scheme. And the cognitive system is akin to a digital coding scheme. According to Harnad: "The CP phenomenon can be seen as an analog-to-digital transformation that recodes a continuous region of physical variation into a discrete, labeled equivalence class" (Harnad, 1987b, p. 4). Circle 2, as it is conceptualized in Figure 12.4, portrays this conversion process as a channel similar to Shannon's communication (information) channel (from Part I).

Figure 12.4 diagrams the transducing operations that occur inside Circle 2 in response to an unfamiliar external environmental stimulus that does not meet the expectations of the user's perceptual/cognitive system. According to our previous discussion of Minsky's frame theory in Part I, the expectation for any feature or aspect of the stimulus object (or event or situation) is categorized within a range of

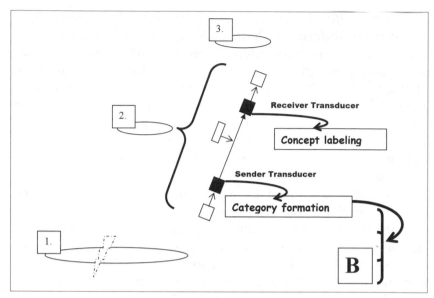

Figure 12.4   Categorization to conceptualization process using environmental stimulus as start of information need, with "B" referring to the lower half of Figure 12.7

likely alternatives called the set, although the most likely (most frequent) signal in the expectation set is the default setting for the feature or aspect of the object, event, or situation.

Let us now look at the first part of this conversion more closely, specifically the categorization transducer shown as the sender transducer in Figure 12.4. In the lower right corner of Figure 12.4, we indicate the sender transduction process with the four-pronged symbol we have used throughout the book to indicate a generic four-member set. According to Harnad, "Every category is based on a specific context of alternatives" (1987b, p. 23). This is for four reasons, which Harnad states as:

1. "The context of confusable alternatives determines the minimum quantity of information that will be required to discriminate reliably among them" (Harnad, 1987a, p. 541).

2. "Categories and their representations can only be provisional and approximate, relative to the alternatives encountered to date, rather than 'exact'" (p. 535).

3. "There is also no such thing as an absolute 'feature,' only those features that are invariant within a particular context of confusable alternatives" (p. 535).

4. "Without this representative sample of the relevant, confusable complement of a category, the highly underdetermined search for features [in unfamiliar thus unexpected environmental stimulus detection] may never converge (i.e., it may never yield reliable, successful categorization performance)" (Harnad, 1987b, p. 23).

We emphasize the importance of the set of confusable or likely alternatives. The categorization of an unfamiliar or unexpected environmental signal must be accomplished while keeping in mind a range of alternative explanations for the stimulus feature or aspect being categorized if the process is 1) to enable detection of the change and 2) to begin (via labeling the stimulus for symbolic system processing leading to organism action) the human organism's adaptation to even the slightest change in the environment.

The categorization process in the sender transducer consists of two subprocesses. According to Harnad, "CP is defined by the discrimination and identification function" (Harnad, 1987b, p. 4):

1. *Discrimination* [matching] requires analog stimulus traces for relative comparisons and for other analog operations (Harnad, 1987a, p. 544). These representations need not—indeed cannot—be categorical.

2. *Identification* [invariant features] requires a feature detector that reliably picks out the features distinguishing the members of a category from confusable nonmembers (Harnad, 1987b, p. 22). ... *Successful categorization depends on* finding the critical features on the basis of which reliable, correct performance can occur. These will depend on the range of confusable alternatives involved, the specific contrasts to be made, and the invariant features that will reliably subserve successful categorization (Harnad, 1987a, p. 540).

We will spend some time defining each of these processes, which are diagrammed in Figures 12.5, 12.6, and 12.7. We have divided these processes into the Discrimination and Identification processes of categorization.

In Figure 12.5, the underlying thrust of the figure is that all sensory processes are continuous and are therefore on a continuum. This is because, as Harnad states:

> In other words, in CP there is a quantitative discontinuity in discrimination at the category boundaries of a physical continuum, as measured by a peak in discriminative acuity at the transition region for the identification of members of adjacent categories. (Harnad, 1987b, p. 3)

Because of the rapidly decaying sensory trace, the human perceptual system must rapidly make decisions about the received stimulus signal; the sensory system is required to rapidly label the stimulus with a verbal label (Harnad, 1987b, p. 13). This rapid labeling is, in the early stages, effectuated by two representational systems that occur or nearly occur at the same time: Discrimination and Identification.

In Figure 12.5, two categories, Category A and Category B, are possible for an incoming environmental stimulus. The stimulus must go through the process of discrimination in order to be identified as either Category A or Category B.

In Figure 12.6, *discrimination* is shown as an "in/out process" where stimulus features are compared to an iconic mediating image inside the user's working memory, which is the sensory system's expectation of the category the stimulus should be classified in. It is

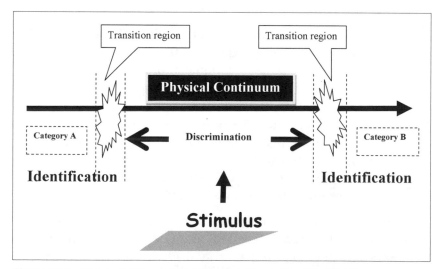

Figure 12.5   Discrimination and Identification in category identification

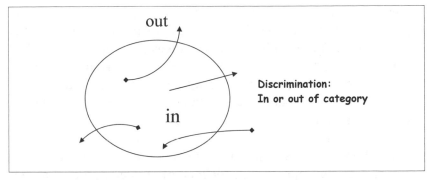

Figure 12.6   Discrimination process: in and out

a matching process, resulting in matching the user's category image in memory to the environmental stimulus signal that has just entered the user's sensory system.

In Figure 12.7, *identification* is defined as the human sensory system identifying what it deems to be salient and invariant features of the stimulus, so that the stimulus can be effectively categorized for use by the human organism. The human organism accomplishes this identification by producing from memory a prototype of the category the organism expects is the correct one, based on past experience (Rosch, 1973). The categorization of the new stimulus in the identification phase is above all the matching of the stimulus's salient features with the salient features of the sensory system's prototype for that category. The salient features of a category are not "necessary and sufficient," according to Rosch, but rather these categories "depend on properties [of the category] that are generally true" (Medin and Rips, 2005, p. 40). A prototype category consists of features of either an ideal or typical (most frequent) case of the category (Harnad, 1987b, p. 19). If the new environmental stimulus has "enough characteristic properties" of the prototype category from memory (i.e., the family resemblance to the prototype is sufficient) then the organism will identify that the stimulus belongs to that category.

During the identification phase (the important point highlighted in Figure 12.7) is what Harnad calls the production by the organism, rather than a single category suggestion, of the most likely alternative category within a set that includes "confusable alternatives" to the category (Harnad, 1987b, pp. 22–23). These are alternatives that may also be possible given the information context of the stimulus. The continuum aspect of perceptual categorization means that not just the expected category identification but also adjacent categories are produced during the identification phase of the processing of the new stimulus. These confusable alternatives are what the organism determines are adjacent categories, or the most likely/possible alternatives if the most likely category is not the right one. The set of confusable alternatives operationally defines the information context of the specific stimulus (Harnad, 1987a, p. 544).

Figure 12.7 illustrates that the objective of the identification is to identify the invariant and salient features of the stimulus signal. It is "context sensitive," operationally defined by Harnad as the set of "relevant and confusable alternative categories" (Harnad, 1987a, p. 552), which is "confusion-resolv[ed]" in the identification process. We indicate this in the figure with the defaults (the black dots) selected for each of the four features, represented by the four-pronged symbol utilized throughout the book to represent the set of likely or possible alternatives. The resulting categorical representation of the stimulus, however, is still mostly in analog form, though digitization into symbolic form has begun. Figure 12.7 shows portions of Figures 12.4 (the "B" refers the reader to a larger view of the process), Figure 12.5 (for Category A), and Figure 12.6 ("in and out").

The category identification of a new environmental stimulus is underdetermined, allowing for maximum flexibility with 1) identifying a stimulus as to its category, and 2) revision of the organism's

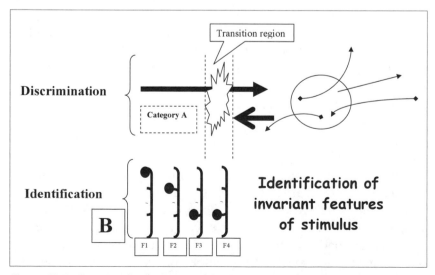

Figure 12.7   The identification phase, with F1–F4 referring to Features 1 to 4

prototype for its categories to take advantage of the latest environmental information on a category. According to adaptation-level theory, a discordant attribute of a category that is repeatedly presented to the subject changes the attribute value so that it is at a midpoint in the range of variation (Harnad, 1987b, p. 17). Therefore, the prototype is constructed so that it is in a constant state of being able to be adapted to changes in the environment.

The production during the identification phase of a set of "confusable alternatives" pertains to properties of a category as well. The confusable alternative set contains the variants of the prototype on a continuum, from features or properties of the category that have been predetermined as salient and invariant features of the feature or property of the category. By invariants, we mean not in the absolute sense but only "sufficient to sub-serve reliable categorization" (Harnad, 1987b, p. 23). In Figure 12.7, we place these predetermined invariant and salient features in the center of Category A, but they are on a continuum. The continuum indicates maximum flexibility for the category property. Rarer features of a property of the category are placed on the periphery of the category continuum. For the category "bird" and the property "can fly," for example, a rare feature of the property of the category "bird" is a bird that cannot fly: an ostrich. The confusable alternatives in the set for this property allow for the flexibility of including "ostrich" in the bird category.

The second transducer shown in Figure 12.4 is the receiver transducer near the top of the indicated channel. Here, the perceptual system transduces the categories into labeled form, the beginnings of conceptualization:

> Finally, the labels of the bounded CP categories provide
> the elementary terms for a *third representational system,*
> *the symbolic descriptions* of natural language (and
> perhaps also of the "language of thought"). (Harnad,
> 1987b, p. 22)

Harnad's CP theory is concerned with categorization, but, he believes, "categorical perception may provide the groundwork for category cognition" (Harnad, 1987a, p. 558). Category cognition is the beginning of conceptualization of the perceptual and analog signal into "digital" or symbolic form; it is a conversion process (from iconic to symbolic representation systems), requiring a transducer. However, conversion to the symbolic representation system is done in a series of steps, the latter steps we define as the Circle 2–3 stage of the user obtaining information from the user's own information sources in response to an unfamiliar environmental stimulus such as unfamiliar information in a results list. We discuss these later conversions in the next section.

12.3.2 Circle 2 to Circle 3

The previous section described the Circle 1 to Circle 2 information flow of an environmental stimulus being processed by the individual's sensory system. Circle 2 converted the analog signal transmitted to it from the environment, represented by Circle 1, into semidigital form. Digital form means the language of thought, of which there are various theories that we will discuss later. Once in semidigital form, for example, the beginnings of propositional statements about the stimulus, the original environmental stimulus is now ready to be incorporated into the individual's symbolic system. Circle 3's processing of the original environmental stimulus is a key stage for our theory of information need. As we will explain, it is at this point in the processing that the individual can effectively conduct an information search in a Pre-focus stage of performing a task, solving a problem, and so on. We have thus far in Part II operationally defined this ability to act as selection: The users of the information system are able, via Circle 3's processing, to select which aspect of their topic they now need to investigate.

This section describes the Circle 2 to Circle 3 information flow to the symbolic system of the individual, again modeling it on Shannon's concept of a communication channel between the two circles, the concept of a message, its conversion to signal form via transducers, and the concept of transducers at both the sender and receiver ends of the channel performing the conversion. During the transmission over the channel, "noise" causes information to drop out of the signal. However, when it is received by Circle 3's transducer, the transducer's algorithms can compensate for this lost information. The Circle 3 transducer converts the signal back into message form, enabling it to be, in Circle 3's associationism network, inserted into the individual's symbolic system.

In Figure 12.8, we diagram the information flow between Circles 2–3. The category representation system discussed in the previous section for Circle 2 sends a signal to Circle 3, the individual's symbolic system, which we define as an associationism network. We define the function of the Circle 2 to 3 information system as the insertion of the

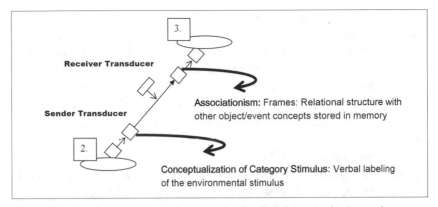

Figure 12.8 Shannon's model of communication flow from sender to receiver using Circles 2 to 3

environmental stimulus into the individual's symbolic system—the memory organization of concepts. Circle 2 is conversion or decoding into categorization and also the beginnings of conceptualization. Circle 3 is digital encoding into the symbolic system of the Association Wheel.

12.3.3 Circle 2

In Circle 2, the environmental stimulus has been categorized to a semidigital state. Circle 2, as per the previous section, is primarily responsible for categorization. Circle 2's transducer now converts the semidigitized, categorized form of the originating environmental stimulus into concepts for transmission to Circle 3.

In this book we make a primary distinction between categories and concepts. In Harnad's (1987a, b) terminology, we can think of categories as how a person receives and does the preliminary transformational work on a stimulus from the environment, so that the stimulus can be understood and perhaps used by the individual to his or her advantage in a social grouping or as part of a species that needs to be aware of and adapt to changes in the environment. However, a category is not in a form that is usable or useful to the human reasoning system, which is in the cognitive or conceptual realm. In Harnad's (1987a, b) terminology, the stimulus at the categorization stage is in analog form and must be converted to digital form in order to be received, understood, and utilized by the human reasoning system. The human reasoning system is concept-based.

Concepts are mental representations of categories that "refer" to the category (Medin and Rips, 2005, p. 37). The analogy is to a telephone call: The sound waves of the human voice have to be converted by the telephone's transducer into digitized form (bits and bytes, 0s and 1s), for transmission as a signal to the receiver—the person whom you are calling. This process involves a conversion from one energy source to another energy form. We will illustrate this energy conversion process later in Part II.

A concept labeling of the category classifies it in a large system of knowledge organization in the user's memory, enabling the individual to make links to further stored knowledge and to generate new knowledge to be applied to the performance of a task or solving a problem. Medin and Rips (2005) give the example of the role that category conversion to concepts plays in human reasoning, referring to the concept "flashlight." The category for this is "cylindrical object." An individual recognizes a cylindrical object, registers it in his or her sensory system, and processes it through Circle 2 into a category. Remember that category processing involves some top-down knowledge transfer (see previous section); and that a category, as we define the process of categorical perception in the previous section, is processed into a semidigital form.

The individual recognizes and registers in the visual system a cylindrical object, and has categorized it based on the stimulus object's invariant and salient features (Circle 2). These features may include 1) a long metal or plastic casing, 2) a clear glass- or plastic-encased light bulb or some source of light, and 3) a switch on the casing, or some similar feature that indicates "on/off." The person's conceptual system then labels the cylindrical object a "flashlight." The original stimulus object is immediately inserted inside the person's symbolic system, in some sort of knowledge organization system, which enables the person to understand and link together the cylindrical object's parts, how they function together, and so forth. The placement of the concept "flashlight" inside the person's knowledge organization system may be hierarchical in some way, which supports inductive and deductive reasoning (Medin and Rips, 2005). Relations between concepts may include substitutes for battery-powered flashlights, other functions of a flashlight (as a weapon, for example), and so on. Relational concepts may include instantiating planning schemes linked to the label "flashlight" in the person's memory structure (Barsalou, 1983). If the person is in a dark location, the label "flashlight" brings up previous experiences with this concept, and these experiences, attached to the concept label, suggest solutions to problems (i.e., how to utilize the flashlight to locate a light in the room or to find a way out). Concept labeling also enables communication of ideas to others, thus extending the user's information search to external information sources for a task or problem.

12.3.4 Circle 3

Circle 3 receives in its transducer the "concept" signal sent by Circle 2 where, as illustrated in Figure 12.8, the concept label is inserted into the person's symbolic system. The human symbolic system (or human reasoning system) corresponds to how information is organized in human memory. "[M]emory organization corresponds to meaningful relations between concepts," according to Medin and Rips (2005, p. 39). Identifying a category with a concept name is accomplished, according to Bruner, Goodnow, and Austin (1956), by inserting the category into a symbolic system.

There have been numerous theories about the structure of human memory organization (for a review, see Medin and Rips, 2005). Associationism (Anderson and Bower, 1973) is an enormously influential theory of memory organization with a long history in information science and computer science. In philosophy, associationism's roots go back to Aristotle's essay *On Memory and Reminiscence* (Anderson and Bower, 1973, p. 16). In the 1930s and 1940s when the internet was first being thought about by people like Vannevar Bush, the dominant paradigm for human thinking/reasoning research was associationism. Other paradigms were Gestaltism, behaviorism, structuralism, and functionalism (Houston and Harmon, 2007). Although it has lost ground in the last few decades (Medin and Rips, 2005, p. 39) to, for example, semantic network theory (Collins and Quillian, 1969) and family resemblance theory (Rosch, 1973), associationism remains an influential theory today in neural network research (Cao, Liang, and Lam 2004), in information science (Houston and Harmon, 2007), and in computer science (e.g., Google's wonder wheel and AquaBrowser's word cloud). The two principal constructs of associationism are that human memory is composed of *ideas* and that these ideas are connected in the human memory system in an associative network (Plotkin, 2004). This results in the pivotal associationism notion that "one idea will elicit another" in the associative network that constitutes human memory (Anderson and Bower, 1973, p. 24).

We illustrate the mechanisms of associationism using Anderson and Bower's (1973) phase-approach associative memory theory. In the first phase, an environmental probe sets in motion a *matching* process between the probe and memory, which establishes a "correspondence between the current input or probe and some piece of the associative structure in memory" (Anderson and Bower, 1973, p. 238). The matching process consists of a *"cue-dependent probabilistic search"* of the "associative network" (Raaijmakers and Shiffrin, 1981, p. 93). A probability-based matching system of this sort establishes a *best match* rather than a perfect match system. Because a best-match matching system allows for imperfections, it produces what is called a search set to commence processing of the environmental probe or stimulus (Ratcliff, 1978). The best-match search set is established for the initiating probe, after which a second mental process *identifies* 1) how much of the matched associations in the person's memory structure "is in fact useable for encoding the current input," and 2) whether "unwarranted conceptualizations" are occurring in the matching process that should be deleted (Anderson and Bower, 1973, pp. 237, 243–245). We note here that, according to this associative memory theory, the identifying process weeds out unusable and/or unwarranted associations from consideration.

This brief description of associative memory theory indicates its similarity to the process of a stimulus's intake by the human memory system. However, we focus here on the organization of human knowledge according to associative memory theory. We define Circle 3 as this associative network memory structure, which we call the Association Wheel, illustrated in Figure 12.9.

The Association Wheel visualizes the user's organization of concepts, both innate (e.g., color, faces) and learned through experience with the environment, that the user associates together. There are many Association Wheels stored in memory. We link this conceptualization of human memory network with other similar conceptions of memory organization: schemas, frames, knowledge structures, mental models, and more. All these memory organization theories posit the notion that humans are guided in their flow through the environment by frames or some other kind of structure that unifies our perceptual and cognitive interaction with the environment and the world.

These Association Wheels form the user's memory structure in a linked network of concepts. When the user is in a Pre-focus information search, the user does not have a strong Association Wheel or

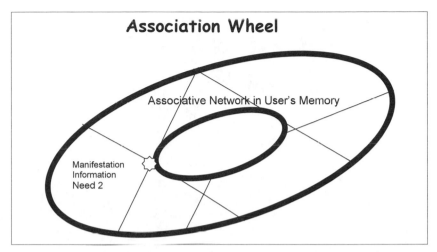

Figure 12.9   The Association Wheel, representing how we think by association

information need frame, so a more general topic has to suffice until focus is reached and a strong Association Wheel information need frame is instantiated.

CHAPTER 13

A Review of the User's Pre-Focus Information Search

In Part II, we have operationalized the user's information need when the user is in Pre-focus information search while the user is perusing the results list. The user is guided by an Association Wheel information need frame that is a general topic in nature—the full information need frame will not be instantiated fully until the user achieves a focus (see Chapter 8 for a full description). We have operationalized the theory in terms of information flow from the environmental stimulus initiation of the information need in Circle 1 up through Circles 2 and 3. Therefore, we assume when the user is in a Pre-focus information search and is perusing the results list that the final Circles 4 and 5 are not yet instantiated. There are two separate information behaviors emanating from this key difference between the Pre-focus stage of information need described here and the Focusing and Post-focus stages of information need described in the next chapters.

First of all, the user's information behavior is more free-flowing and disparate in the Pre-focus information search, as the user investigates different aspects of the general topic. The user is constructing the Association Wheel information need frame, picking up topic information bit by bit. In the Pre-focus information search, the user is guided by the selection concept developed in information science starting with Cutter and fully developed for the internet age by Vannevar Bush in his conceptualization of a memex machine where the user "selects the next item he/she will investigate" based on the associations a textual fragment stimulates in the user's mind.

The general topic Association Wheel information need frame utilized by the user in a Pre-focus information search while perusing the results list is a form of conceptual system representation. These conceptual system representations of a topic space have been investigated under various other names, including: mental models,

cognitive maps, concept maps, and mind maps. Like all these formu-
lations of the internal mental representations humans utilize to guide
them as they interact with their environment, the conceptual system
represented by the general-topic Association Wheel is an internal
representation of the target topic space, a conceptual system stand-
ing in for the real, or represented world (Hirtle and Heidorn, 1993).
The user's internal conceptual system may not correspond at all to
the real world (i.e., the topic domain of the search) and thus the
Association Wheel utilized by this user may be in need of major revision. The way of facilitating major revision in the Association Wheel
is to build in the underdetermination, which we have represented
throughout this book via the concept of the four-pronged symbol
representing the confusable alternatives in the set.

In Figure 13.1, we diagram the position of the user conducting a
Pre-focus search while perusing the results list. We hypothesize that
the form of this person's information need is stilted, ending at Circle
3. This is in contrast with the full Circle 1 to Circle 5 fullness of a complete, instantiated information need, which takes place due to a
Focusing procedure. We will describe a ful Focusing process involving
all Circles 1–5 in the following chapters. Here, we describe the Pre-
focus information search only.

In Figure 13.1, the method of conducting a Pre-focus information
search with an incomplete version of a fully instantiated information
need frame is Circle 3's Association Wheel. The Association Wheel
information need frame allows the user to carry out useful information search through its facilitation of user selection. Selection is, as
Vannevar Bush defined it, the ability of the user to "select" the next
item or aspect of the topic to investigate, stimulated by the associations produced in the user's mind when reading informative text. In
Figure 13.1, we summarize this selection process in the diagram with
a four-pronged symbol that operationalizes the Harnad concept of
the set of confusable and likely alternatives. The individual is now
capable of making a "symbolic response" (Kendler and Kendler,
1962), *which is the selection of the next item or aspect of the topic to
investigate in the information search.*

The new aspects of the topic the user sees in the results list causes
the user's Association Wheel to constantly shift during the information search. In the results list, the user sees pieces of information that
touch on an aspect of the topic and decides to pursue investigation of
them. In Figure 13.2, the Association Wheel in the user's memory

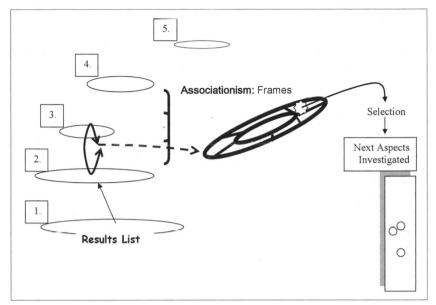

Figure 13.1 Associationism, selection from the set of confusable and likely alternatives, and the resulting "selection" of the next aspects to be investigated by the user

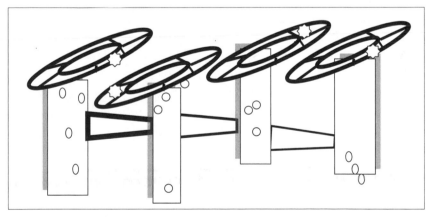

Figure 13.2 Association Wheel: a constantly shifting, evolving process during information search

directs this continuously shifting and evolving selection of which aspects the user next *selects* to investigate.

Figure 13.1 and Figure 13.2 show the user's information search behavior while making a selection when only Circles 1–3 are involved. This defines the Pre-focus stage of information search.

Focusing and Post-focus searching involve further processes, which will be described in the next chapters.

We are now ready to set the stage for a description of how the user in a Pre-focus information search who is perusing the results list can go to the next circle level (Circles 4 and 5), to instantiate his or her full information need during the Focusing phase (as outlined in Chapter 8). The instantiated information need frame then carries the user through to task completion or problem solution in an efficient manner, with the full capability of making relevance judgments based on this information need.

CHAPTER 14

How Information Need Works in a Focusing Search

In Chapters 10 through 13, we described how the user's Association Wheel and the concept of selection governs Pre-focus search. The user's Circle 3 Association Wheel selects which item the user will decide to investigate next. We defined the information flow process leading to Circle 3 in terms of Shannon's model of communication (information) flow discussed in Part I. The Shannon model operationalizes the information content of the information flow situation as it flows through a channel via the concept of the set—the set of likely alternatives, which we have also described as the user's "expectation set." As previously discussed in Part II, Harnad (1987b, p. 23) adds the word "confusable," making the expectation set the set of likely and confusable alternatives, thus creating the sense of under-determinedness necessary for our theory of information need to be sensitive to changes in the environment, to enable the user to. This means that the user's mind is in expectation mode when conducting an information search utilizing an information system, but never reaches the level of 100 percent certainty about what he or she has just received. There is always uncertainty, which could, for some reason in the particular information context, slip the probability calculations to another member of the set. Members of the set apparently can be, by definition, peripheral to the topic at hand. This is an important point to underline, and we will refer to it again in subsequent sections.

In this chapter, we describe how information need works in Focusing Search, which implicates Circles 4 and 5. We focus on how an aspect of a topic turns into a feature of the user's information need frame. Once Circles 4 and 5 are involved in the information need, the full information need frame of the user is instantiated.

In Part I, we defined full information need frame instantiation by describing the various levels of information need, specifically the deepest, unconscious level of need, via Taylor's four-level conceptualization, Q1–Q4. A need related to writing a report at work or an essay at school, even though these work- and school-related needs don't seem to be existential, are existential at their deepest level. We have shown in Part II that a reduced form of information need can serve as an adequate information need frame for a user in a Pre-focus stage of performing a task or solving a problem. But to achieve focus in performing the task or to solve the problem, a person must engage his or her deepest level of need.

As we defined this deepest Q1 level of need in Part I, information science must go to the root of all human information need: the need to detect changes in the environment, react to them, and thus survive. It is our thesis that only by considering this deepest level of need can we get at the neurological basis for information need: how it works and why it works. For this reason, we have gone to evolutionary psychology. Evolutionary psychology has approached these questions and offered tentative possibilities for how information need operates, given that the why of information need is to detect and adapt to changes in the human environment. We look to evolutionary psychology's take on information need to elucidate Circle 4, belief, and Circle 5, the neurological basis of information need.

To illustrate how information need works when Circles 4 and 5 are joined to the information need frame, we refer to data from a study of PhD history students researching/writing their dissertations (Cole, 1994a). This example illustrates how the instantiation of information need's deepest level works from the beginning, starting from when these people are in a Pre-focus, exploratory stage of the information need, all the way to the moment when they achieve focus, and their full Q1–Q4 information need is instantiated. We have previously reported the data for this study (Cole, 1998; Cole, 2000a; Cole, 2000b). Here, however, for the first time, we utilize this data to illustrate in real terms the theory of information need outlined in this book.

14.1 Circles 4–5: Belief System(s) and the Neurological Determination of Human Reasoning

It is our hypothesis that Focusing occurs when Circle 3 "invites" information flow and knowledge formation from Circles 4 and 5. With this information flow and knowledge formation influx, the user's information need is instantiated as per Chapter 8. Circles 4 and 5 were discussed in Part I. Here, we briefly review them before going on to the empirical data from Cole (1994a).

Circle 4 is the belief system(s) of the user. The belief system has both positive and negative effects on information need. The negative effect is a prejudice of the user which blocks him or her from recognizing potentially valuable information in the social environment. Rokeach calls these "closed systems of thinking and believing" (1960, p. 69). The positive effect is the different perspective a belief system gives to the user. It is a global perspective. The belief system includes minute things like: I believe my enemy has X and Y characteristics. These characteristics are associated, then, with danger or at least antipathy. As an example, a prejudice against a group that the user considers an enemy group creates an acutely sensitive warning system for the user, potentially protecting the user's life. We can see how this belief system maximized the warning benefit throughout human history, although perhaps not so much today.

Another type of belief system is the belief in time travel or parallel time frames. Rokeach (1960, p. 48) gives the example of a camera being able to photograph heat waves of cars on a parking lot, a few hours after they had been driven off. If this heat wave camera was presented as a camera that could photograph the past, it would then introduce an avenue of research to someone with the correctly attuned belief system—i.e., someone who believes a camera can photograph the past (with special lenses that can photograph ruins of ancient settlements under the ground).

It has been recognized in information science research that uncertainty is associated with novel or unfamiliar information context, including the human organism receiving an unexpected and unfamiliar environmental stimulus signal. Kuhlthau (1993) states that there are two types of uncertainty: cognitive and affective uncertainty (Wilson, Ford, Foster, Ellis, and Spink, 2002, p. 712), with cognitive uncertainty coming first. In other words, we have to develop a belief about the incoming environmental stimulus in front of us before we can develop a feeling for it—of fear, repulsion, sadness, empathy, and so on. In belief theory, this would be restated as: The user has to believe he or she feels uncertain before he or she actually feels the uncertainty.

The belief system could be a way into the Focusing process resulting in information need instantiation, as per our theory of information need. There is some evidence for this in the evidence from the empirical study we discuss in the next sections of the book. We believe this is a very interesting avenue of thought, which we briefly refer to in Figure 14.1. Figure 14.1 utilizes the positive feedback illustrated in Figures 6.5, 7.2, 7.3, and 7.4 from Part I, where an unexpected environmental stimulus signal receives amplification. After investigating alternatives from the expectation set via thinking and information seeking activities, if the user can believe one of the alternatives in the set is true, in terms of his or her belief systems (for example, over the 50 percent mark as indicated in Figure 14.1), then this may lead to eventual instantiation of the user's information need frame.

In the last 5 years, information science has begun to examine information search within the broad framework of evolutionary psychology to better describe how and why humans conduct information search (Spink, 2010). Evolutionary psychology asks the question: How does a person recognize a gap or change in the social or physical environment which sets off the process leading to adaptation? We get some idea of this process by comparing humans to an unsuccessful

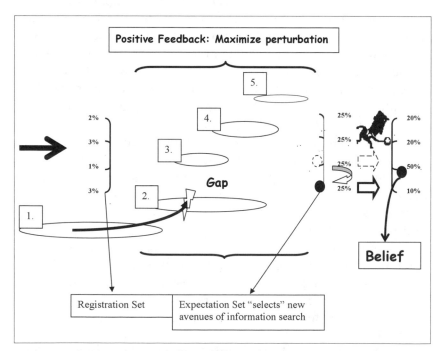

Figure 14.1   Introduction of belief systems, eventually leading to the information need instantiation process

but related species, the Neanderthals, who did not recognize and adapt to changes in their environment, and so did not survive (for further discussion of this point, see Cole, 2008).

It is hypothesized that humans and Neanderthals started from a roughly similar cognitive architecture during the overlap period of the two, evolutionary-distinct species. There are various hypotheses about the modern human adaptation that enabled humans to survive where the Neanderthals did not. One is the "Big Leap" hypothesis which states that human survival was due to a chance mutation in human cognition occurring roughly 35,000 years ago (Mithin, 1996; for discussion, see Spink and Cole, 2006). A contrary hypothesis of human cognitive development is sometimes referred to as the unitary or encephalization hypothesis (Donald, 1991), which states that modern human cognition followed a more normal evolutionary development tied to the gradual increase in human brain size, possibly driven by human intergroup competition for limited resources (Alexander, 1990). Consistent with this second hypothesis, Wynn and Coolidge (2004) attribute the adaptation in human behavior to a moderate increase in the size of human working memory, leading to what they call enhanced working memory (EWM) (see also Martín-Loeches, 2006; for a review see Baddeley, 2001).

Pre-EWM humans, like their Neanderthal competitors, could only focus their limited working memory attention capacity on the most probable path to successful task solution performance, based on past experience with the same task (Wynn and Coolidge, 2004); but this episodic or strategic-based cognition was ineffective when the environmental stimulus was unfamiliar or novel.

EWM enabled humans

1. To juggle multiple retrieval structures in working memory at the same time, including both the known, habitual retrieval/solution structure as well as other less probable retrieval structures, allowing the potential for innovative solution responses to the problem at hand. The alternatives included memory sequences from other areas of expertise and other experiences of everyday life (Wynn and Coolidge, 2004; see also Spink and Cole, 2006).

2. To much better focus on one solution structure alternative over others that were being considered in working memory, which led to

A. The reduction of failures of goal maintenance when performing a task or solving a problem (Wynn and Coolidge, 2004), which could previously occur as a result of interference from previous goal processing (retroactive interference) or interference from competing concurrent goals (proactive interference) (Kane and Engle, 2002), and

B. The ability to focus in on novel retrieval solution/responses to the problem or cue at hand rather going with the tried and true method from past experience (Wynn and Coolidge, 2004; see also Conway, Cowan, and Bunting, 2001; Duncan, Emslie, Williams, Johnson, and Freer, 1996; Kane, Bleckley, Conway, and Engle, 2001).

The new ability of post-EWM humans to "generatively" adapt to unfamiliar environmental stimuli led to new and different kinds of knowledge structures that evolved over time; enabling humans to more effectively modify their behavior and adapt to changing environmental conditions. Without EWM on the other hand, Neanderthals "may have had trouble adjusting to novel conditions, particularly those that might have required new ways of behaving outside the range of their individual expert abilities" (Wynn and Coolidge, 2004, p. 477).

Circles 1 to 5: An Example of How Information Need Works

15.1 The Study

Here in Chapter 15, we illustrate how information need works from the 5 Circles perspective by citing data from a study first reported in Cole (1994a). In this study, forty-five history PhD candidates from six universities in northern England were interviewed about how they became informed while researching/writing their dissertations. Data were collected and analyzed utilizing the grounded theory methodology of Glaser and Strauss (1967). The analysis of the data showed that the process by which the PhD students became informed could be divided into Picture-formation, Jigsaw-Pieces-formation, and Jigsaw-Coming-Together-formation. The Picture-formation stage is the beginning stage of the thesis-researching/writing process where the students, freshly enrolled in their program, had to read and learn about their topic area. The Jigsaw-Pieces-formation was when the conceptual nature of the thesis researching/writing began to take shape; the pieces correspond to issues, problems, and concepts the PhD student could see were of interest and would probably wind up in their thesis. The Jigsaw-Coming-Together-formation was when they formed the thesis of the research/writing, which tied together the pieces of the Jigsaw into some kind of structure.

The key point we wish to emphasize in citing this study is the Jigsaw-Pieces-formation process. One of the subjects in the Cole (1994a) study gives a succinct overview of the 1) Picture and 2) Jigsaw, which can be roughly defined, respectively, as 1) the background reading for the dissertation, and 2) the conceptual framework of the PhD student's dissertation. The Jigsaw must, as the first PhD student

145

we cite states, be kept in an underdetermined state, so that it can react to sudden changes in what the student is reading—the student's "textual" environment.

15.2 Data Analysis

We begin the data analysis by referring to a subject who describes the relationship between Picture and Jigsaw. The title of this PhD student's dissertation was "Kinship and Community in Yorkshire, 1500 to 1700." A turning point in this student's research, affecting one-third of his thesis "at the very highest conceptual level," occurred as a result of reading an anthropological textbook about kinship in 20th-century Papua New Guinea. The student then went back to books he had previously read, and found he was reading them with a new eye:

> For the same reason I keep rereading things because you go through again and you find something you thought was irrelevant the time before but this time it seems relevant because you've picked up new information, and it's rather like boarding a Jigsaw, you keep taking bits out of a box and kind of slotting them into your Picture, and your conceptual Jigsaw is getting bigger all the time, and occasionally you find you've, very like a Jigsaw, you're doing a bit of blue sky at the top and you've done it all incorrectly and you got to kinda take it to pieces and put it back somewhere else. (Cole 1994a, Interview 34, Disk 3, page 42, line 17)

In Figure 15.1, we diagram the Picture to Jigsaw-Pieces-formation. There are obvious similarities between Picture-formation and the Pre-focus stage of information search described earlier in this book. Instead of "aspects," we label the Jigsaw Pieces "Feature 1," "Feature 2," and so on in Figure 15.1 to underscore this similarity. In the Pre-focus stage, the user investigates a shifting or evolving series of features or aspects of the topic. The Jigsaw-Pieces-formation is roughly equivalent to the Focusing stage thus far described in this book. Citing data taken from Cole (1994a, pp. 277–289), we go through these stages and recode the data into the theory of information need presented in this book. However, in the study we will now cite, because the objective of the study was to model a single information process for each subject, the data do not illustrate more than one

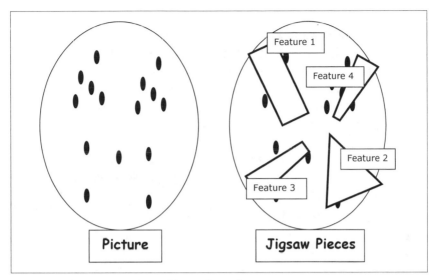

Figure 15.1   Picture to Jigsaw-Pieces-formation

Jigsaw-Pieces-formation at a time (i.e., the Focusing stage was not the objective of Cole, 1994a).

15.2.1 The Picture

The Picture is the background knowledge a PhD student must build up about his or her topic area. It is from the Picture that the issues, problems, and thesis for the PhD dissertation emerge. The Picture also controls what the PhD candidate sees in the material he or she is reading.

In the following data fragment taken from the interview with a PhD student whose thesis was entitled "Political Opposition and Republicanism in England, 1672 to 1683," the PhD student describes the background reading as enabling him to see "links" to radicalism in a connected group of supposedly moderate "Republicans":

> I looked at this journal myself in Cambridge and it was marvelous, … [I] could get so much evidence of Republican links and Republican this, that, and the other, not just from that, you need to have the background of what I'd already researched to know, that's probably why he [the author of the second source J. R. Jones] didn't see it partly because he hadn't had this background of research

in Republicanism, of seeing names and things, and seeing
the same names crop up in this journal. But it was very
exciting because I had plenty of proof, more proof now of
these Republican interactions within this club, so that was
marvelous; I was ecstatic over that. So that was pivotal in
the sense that it added a whole new dimension to my PhD.
(Interview 14, Disk 2, page 47, line 29)

For defining the Picture, our next series of quotes, from a PhD student doing a thesis on the political history of Lycia and its relations
with foreign powers from 545 to 362 B.C., refers to the nondiscrimi-
nate note-taking at the beginning of researching/writing his PhD:

These were my copious, neatly written notes I did in the first
three or four months of my work. I don't take notes anything
like this [now]. (Interview 8, Disk 1, page 32, line 4)

The reason he gave for the difference in style of note-taking at the
beginning of the research and now at the time of the interview was
not knowing what he was looking for at the beginning of the research:

Well I think now I go in and I know what I'm actually looking for. To an extent, in these, when I was doing this [note-
taking at the beginning of the research], I wasn't quite sure
what I was looking for so I was writing down anything that
might be interesting, that might be useful, let's get all that
down, etc. etc. etc. (Interview 8, Disk 1, page 32, line 19)

For another PhD student doing a dissertation on sociology of the
British Army in the early 19th century, who was in the first year of
researching/writing her dissertation, everything was still relevant. I
had asked her questions that sought to contrast the difference
between the Picture ("interesting") and the Jigsaw ("relevant") reading. She answered:

Interesting but not relevant? Trying to think. Not really, I
was going to say just about everything is relevant because
I'm trying to maintain a larger Picture at a sort of lower
level of volume, as it were, I'm trying to maintain a context
and a much broader Picture, both say other regiments,
other armies, other periods, the whole thing, other areas of

social and economic history. (Interview 40, Disk 4, page 35, line 55)

The Jigsaw-Pieces-formation consist of categorization-conceptualization movements in the process of researching/writing the student's dissertation, where instead of the broad mass of undifferentiated stimuli in reading, lectures attended, and so on, the student begins to see the dissertation as distinct pieces, or categories, that are gradually evolving toward coming together around an argument statement or thesis.

15.2.2 The Picture to Jigsaw-Pieces-formation

At a certain point, the PhD's background Picture conceptually breaks into distinct parts. These parts are the issues, themes, and controversies that the student recognizes are in the dissertation topic. In Figure 15.1 we diagrammed the transition from Picture to Jigsaw-Pieces-formation, with Features 1, 2, 3, and 4 representing the issues, themes, and controversies the student has recognized in the dissertation topic. In the following sections, we describe Jigsaw-Pieces-formation, which is a Focusing stage for the information need of the PhD students researching/writing their dissertation.

15.2.2.1 Circle 1: Stimulus

It is important to emphasize the physical nature of these information-related processes, where the flow of information from the environment goes up through channels of information flow through Circle 1 to Circle 2 to Circle 3. The stimulus is in analog signal form. It is converted by transducers in the series of channels we have previously described linking Circle 1 to Circle 2 to Circle 3. The key channel transducers are in the category-conceptualization conversion that takes place before and after Circle 2, illustrated in Figure 15.2.

These conversion processes are physical processes. The PhD students indicated these conversions with physical expressions. The example from Cole (1994a) we take to illustrate this conversion phenomenon of information flow, which is felt physically by the user, is a PhD student researching/writing a dissertation on the Anglo-French peace negotiations during the French Revolutionary Wars. The orthodox view of these wars was that England was the weaker of the two countries. However, as a result of reading a French government decree, the student concluded that the French government of the

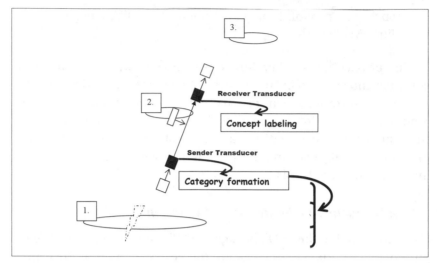

Figure 15.2   The key channel transducers before and after Circle 2

time perceived the relative strength of the two countries differently than modern day historians—the PhD student believed after finding the document that the French were quite frightened by England.

This PhD student begins the following quote by expressing his "disbelief" at what the document seemed to be saying:

> Because I first read it, and then it struck me because it was an important measure which I had never heard, I've never read about in the secondary literature before, so I read it first of all rather disbelievingly, thinking perhaps that I hadn't understood it properly; it was written in French of course so I distrusted my translation, so I remember puzzling over for some time before I realized [what it really was] … what it appeared to be was an order to the Minister of Police to expel foreigners from Paris and every other commune in France within a period of three weeks. (Interview 24, Disk 3, page 60, line 1)

15.2.2.2 Circle 1 to Circle 2: Stimulus to Categorization

The environmental stimulus (Circle 1) begins the process of information flow; in Harnad's (1987a) terms, it is in analog form. The next PhD student illustrates a crucial step in the information flow from

Circle 1 to 2. This is the creation of a set of confusable and likely alternatives that begins the processing of the textual stimulus.

We illustrate the Circle 1 to Circle 2 information flow with a PhD dissertation with the working title "A Survey of Religious Guilds in the Later Middle Ages in the Historical County of Yorkshire, Up to and Including Dissolution." The PhD student's primary source material was several thousand wills written in Latin. The PhD student starts with the textual stimulus that started the information flow—two sheep:

> **Answer:** I think if you start seeing these folks as people it makes you think, it makes you wonder, it makes you think to yourself: two sheep! I mean, this isn't an irrelevancy, but the thought is perhaps almost an irrelevancy, but it's not, because you think: two sheep? Now what does this tell us about this guild that he thought they wanted two sheep? Two sheep indeed that they're not allowed to sell—this was a will I got last week. No, they have to be used for the purposes of the guild and no one's allowed to sell them.

The PhD student then listed answers to his question, "Two sheep?":

> **Answer:** Yes, I thought, Is this the wool they have to use?
> **Question:** Is this the what?
> **Answer:** The wool they have to use or are they supposed to slaughter them for their own needs, I don't know, because of course guilds were, the annual party was quite an important part of [the social function of the guild].
> (Interview 20, Disk 2, page 103, line 8)

Note that the PhD student went into his background reading, the Picture, to find two answers to his question about the two sheep, and found two likely but confusable alternatives, which constitute the expectation set referred to earlier in Part II:

1. "Is this the wool they have to use?"

2. "Or are they supposed to slaughter them [the sheep] for their own needs ... [for] the annual party ... ?"

We give a second example of a PhD student's expectation set, which is the set of confusable and likely alternatives to answer a question

that came up in the student's reading material. In this second example, from a dissertation entitled "Britain's Electoral System in the Early
Nineteenth Century," the PhD student was reading a book by Al
Gorman about corruption in Britain, and suddenly wanted to know
the answer to the question: How do you define corruption? But if you
look closely at the quote, the real initiating textual stimulus for the
information flow is an anomaly in the reasoning of the author the PhD
student was reading, in this author's logic concerning corruption. The
author didn't think "artificially inflat[ing] their expenses," the "their"
being the elected officials, was corruption affecting election results:

> I was certainly reading about corruption, and I was just
> trying to think how should you go about defining the word.
> I think I may have been reading Al Gorman because he was
> making the distinction between corruption by politicians
> and corruption by election officials. So, for example, if the
> returning officer artificially inflates their expenses, in a
> sense you can say that that's corrupt, but they're not affect-
> ing the outcome of the election by inflating their election
> expenses, so he [Gorman] was making this point about
> [how] you have to be careful about who you're talking
> about being corrupt because not all corruption affects the
> outcome of the election, and I think that was what got me
> thinking about, you know, how do you define corruption,
> how do you define bribery, what standards should you be
> using. (Interview 13, Disk 2, page 5, line 17)

The PhD student then stopped reading the Al Gorman book and
began to take notes in a special notebook for this purpose. The notes
related to what the PhD student had read before about election practices in modern day America and Japan:

> I think it was actually not reading but thinking through it
> myself and comparing it with modern times; I mean the
> two things that spring to mind are Japan and America. Now
> the modern Japanese electoral system I would say is cor-
> rupt but I wouldn't say the same thing about the American
> and I think I was comparing what I was reading about 19th
> century Britain with these two modern ones ... because in
> Japan there are lots of things like all the cheap shares for
> politicians, but those are often bribing politicians to carry

out particular policy, so you give the politician cheap
shares, then they say you have a government contract to
the firm. (Interview 13, Disk 2, page 4, line 22)

Whereas in 20th-century America, the politician does not "take"
but rather "gives" in order to be reelected. We examine this more
closely in the following sections.

15.2.2.3 Circle 2: Categorization

The PhD student researching/writing the corruption dissertation categorized the environmental textual stimulus (the Al Gorman gap in
logical reasoning about corruption) in the following way:

In America the type of quotes [about] "corruption" you get
is basically pork barreling, the local senator or congress-
man gets lots of government's money put into the local
constituency without any necessary direct personal gain
for them, although indirect personal gain in that they are
more likely to be reelected and all that fringe benefits that
run off from that. (Interview 13, disk 2, page 4, line 27)

The expectation set of confusable and like alternatives to the originating textual stimulus is two different concepts of corruption:

1. In Japan the corrupt politician "gets" money.

2. In America the corrupt politician gives money
   (government contracts).

15.2.2.3.1 Circle 2: Conceptualization

The PhD student researching/writing the corruption dissertation has
now categorized the initiating environmental textual stimulus in
terms of the expectation set of confusable and likely alternatives. The
student will now read subsequent textual material, and think about
the initiating stimulus in terms of this question-answer set. Notice
that the set is in answer form.

The PhD student believed his topic, the politician in 19th-century
Britain, was similar to the modern-day Japanese form of corruption
in rhetoric, but the same as American corruption in that the corrupt
politician gives rather than "takes" money.

And I was thinking that the rhetoric [in 19th-century Britain] is very much the type you'd expect for Japan. You know it's all this horrible corrupt politicians with money and so on. In fact, if you look at [19th-century Britain], what it is is the politicians are giving out money which is being labeled as corrupt, rather than politicians tak[ing] money. (Interview 13, Disk 2, page 4, line 34)

The conceptualization of the discordance initiated by the Al Gorman gap in logic (the environmental textual stimulus) resulting from the categorization of the environmental signal as "give" and "take" is confused because this is early going in this PhD student's case, but it has something to do with "rhetoric" or something along the lines of different labeling for the same behavior. For some reason (the student didn't know at the time of the interview), 19th-century Britain utilized 20th-century Japanese-style rhetoric, but the actual corruption practices in 19th-century Britain was 20th-century American-style corruption.

15.2.2.4 Circle 3: Insertion Inside Symbolic System
The next PhD dissertation, on European pietism in 18th-century Yorkshire, illustrates information flow entering Circle 3's receiver transducer, where further conceptualization takes place—in Harnad's terminology, the analog signal is further digitized—via insertion into the user's symbolic system, which fully conceptualizes the stimulus.

The PhD student formerly believed that the sect he was studying, called the Moravians, was localized in Formack, which is a settlement in Yorkshire. But then he saw "names" of religious leaders from Formack alongside "names" of international religious leaders:

Now I realize that these names were some of others who were also named who had also been thinking about these ideas and writing about them, and so in the first of these two volumes which I was telling you about, it opened my eyes to the realization that what happened at Formack was even more interesting than I had realized because Formack was reflecting a very wide deep-rooted European movement ... (Interview 29, Disk 3, page 65, line 8). ... In other words what I've discovered in my work so far is less, although this is a highly individual movement, particularly its notions about living in communities, it's far less unique than I had imagined. (Interview 29, Disk 3, page 67, line 5)

In this case, the piece breaking off the Picture to form Jigsaw Pieces is a process which begins with the Picture—background reading done before on pietism—suddenly instantiating as a theme or issue in his dissertation. The Jigsaw Piece is pietism:

> Pietism was there but it was in the background; I was thinking of the institutions, structure, what in fact occurred, so although Pietism was there it was as you might say in the background of my mind. Now I'm reading widely about Pietism, which perhaps I ought to have done earlier, I now see the context. (Interview 29, Disk 3, page 63, line 41)

The Jigsaw Piece that formed in this example is "pietism." The process of Jigsaw-Pieces-formation to categorization, conceptualization, and finally insertion of the concept inside the PhD student's symbolic system can be listed as the following:

1. Background: "Pietism was there," the PhD student said, "but it was in the background." The "background" is the Picture.

2. Stimulus: Then the PhD student happened to read in a secondary work the names of members of the local Moravian sect in Formack he was studying juxtaposed right alongside the names of international religious leaders.

3. Categorization: From this juxtaposition of names in one textual place, the student realized the Moravian movement in Formack was not local but international.

4. Conceptualization: The PhD student widened-out this realization into the Picture. He described that moment, the widening out, as "my thesis deepened" (Interview 29, Disk 3, page 66, line 5).

5. Insertion in student's symbolic system: The "international not local" idea widened into the Picture and fully conceptualized into *Pietism*.

We do not know why or how the PhD student gave the category "international not local" the concept label *pietism*. If he meant the generic "pietism," defined in the dictionary as "pious sentiment" (*Oxford Dictionary of Current English*, 1984, p. 556), then the pietism label came also from the student's Belief System (Circle 4) and Neurological System (Circle 5). Or he could be referring to the specific religious sect called "Pietism" that was going on within the same timeframe (18th century) of his dissertation. But this is not clear so we leave the Circle 4 and 5 implications in the processing and analog-to-digital conversion of information flow until the next section where the data are clearer. In Figure 15.3, we diagram the Association Wheel and Pietism inside the Picture and leave it in Circle 3.

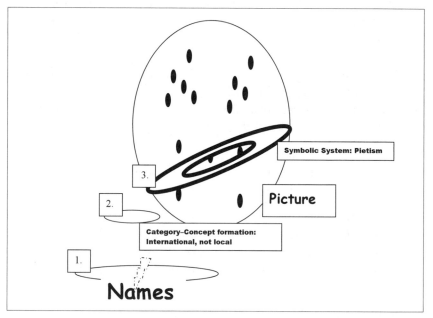

Figure 15.3 Information flow into Symbolic System: Association Wheel inside Picture

15.2.2.5 Circles 4–5: A Complete Information Flow Cycle

In the following example of a student whose dissertation was on the topic of the development of popular politics in two communities in 19th-century England, the environmental stimulus centers on the textual term "bastardy arrears," which is an old British legal term describing a common law marriage where the man is in default of payment for the upkeep of his so-called "bastard" (i.e., out-of-wedlock) children:

> What happened was this: that people would be taken to court for not paying this arrears. But they didn't explain what it was, and couldn't understand, what the hell's a bastardy arrears? (Interview 45, Disk 5, page 27, line 42)

The PhD student widened "bastardy arrears" out in his background reading, the Picture, which he calls the "fit[ting] into a much broader context":

> You see, what I'm saying is that when I get an insight it sort of fits into a much broader context and I start thinking it out gradually over a period of days, you see, and it sort of just comes, but the initial click can be one word and one phrase. (Interview 45, Disk 5, page 27, line 27)

The student defined "bastardy arrears" by reading through law case after law case:

> Apparently what happened was this: that the couple concerned decided to have a trial marriage, well these were usually people who were without fixed income, then if they had children the man agreed to keep the children, and if he said that he was going to break up the common law marriage he would then agree to pay maintenance. Now this worked as long as he was working, if not he then got dragged to court for not paying his maintenance. (Interview 45, Disk 5, page 26, line 1)

The student then widened "common law marriage" into what he had previously read and stored in the Picture, which suddenly became a category of meaningful information—"*informal system of liaisons*" (emphasis added in quote):

> But I discovered from that, there was a whole *informal system of liaisons* that were quite respectable within the working class, a very fluid sort of thing, also the attitude to prostitution then suddenly becomes different, things that people have said then become explicable, this is what I

> mean ... This also explains why you get the rise of the
> Birmingham Temperance Union, because they're not just
> talking about drink or the evils of tobacco smoking or
> breaking the Sabbath, they also go on about shameful con-
> duct, men and women living together outside wedlock,
> but also the attitudes, the mores, the lack of respectability.
> (Interview 45, Disk 5, page 26, line 12, line 21)

We illustrate the complete information flow from this bastardy arrears example in Figure 15.4, overlaying the Association Wheel in Circle 3 onto the PhD student's Picture. This is the symbolic system of the student. In the student's Association Wheel, the student discovered the following associated concepts to "common law marriage": the rise of the Birmingham Temperance Union, which had connected associations: drinking, evils of smoking, breaking Sabbath, and the shameful conduct of men and women living together out of wedlock. The PhD student, when he inserted the conceptualization ("common law marriage") of the category ("informal system of liaisons") into his symbolic system, further conceptualized "common law marriage" into fully digital form: "social camouflage" (in Circle 3). Social camouflage labels the underlying idea, in this student's mind, of common law marriage.

Circles 4 and 5 now come into play. The initiating stimulus "bastardy arrears" widening out into the student's Picture signaled Circles 4 and 5 to send messages, further processing the textual stimulus "bastardy arrears." The student's Belief System (Circle 4), summarized in the term "respectability," and the student's Neurological System, summarized in the sociology theory term "social profile," completed the processing of information flow stimulated by the words "bastardy arrears." The term "social profile" places the information flow into a theoretical framework that may help the PhD student research/write his dissertation. However, the central insight in this bastardy arrears example of information flow is Circle 3, as indicated with the arrows flowing from Circle 4 and 5 to Circle 3, to assist in the processing of the stimulus into the central thesis idea: social camouflage. We indicate Circle 3 as the central production system with an arrow in Figure 15.4.

We summarize this difficult last paragraph in Table 15.1. The point of contention in the analysis presented here is Belief System. The flow of information processing began with the stimulus "bastardy arrears," which we analyze to be that the concept "common law marriage" is an attempt by the lower half of the middle class to gain respectability for their "informal system of liaisons." This is because common law marriage, the student believes, creates "social camouflage" for behavior by making it seem "respectable." There are other interpretations for "bastardy arrears" and the whole system of common law marriage, but this particular PhD student interpreted it in terms of respectability. It is actually a somewhat surprising belief (i.e., against the normal interpretation of common law marriage). The more common interpretation of common law marriage is that it is not a bottom-up system (to gain respectability) but rather a top-down system, created by the state to make order out of the chaos of human social relations that were, in the beginning, outside of the reach of the legal system. We indicate the central importance of the student's symbolic system in Table 15.1. The symbolic system, we hypothesize, is the important processing circle of the PhD student's dissertation in its final form, the central idea of this feature. Not only is Circle 3, the symbolic system where the initiating environmental stimulus is fully converted to digital form (to utilize Harnad's terminology), but it coincides with Rosch's (1973) important observation that humans feel most comfortable entering at the middle level in concept hierarchies such as "Barcelona chair-chair-furniture," for naming objects, for learning by children, and the "correlational structure of features" (see also Medin and Rips, 2005, pp. 40–41). In the present example of a PhD student (Table 15.1 and Figure 15.4), the Symbolic System's "social camouflage" is the most

Table 15.1   Summary of information flow from "bastardy arrears" to a theoretical explanation of it

Circle	Information Processing	PhD Student's Term	Explanation
1	Stimulus	"bastardy arrears"	The initiating "insight"
2	Category	"informal system of liaisons"	The raw categorization of the insight
	Concept	"common law marriage"	A conceptualization in legal terminology
3	**Symbolic System**	**"social camouflage"**	**What is actually going on**
4	Belief System	"respectability" therefore: bottom-up	The student's belief
5	Neurological System – Theoretical Label	"social profile"	Sociological term based in theory

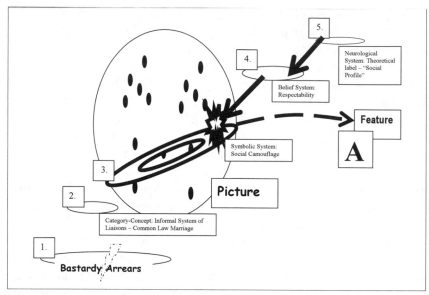

Figure 15.4   Overlaying Association Wheel onto PhD student's Picture (Circle 3), suddenly signaling Circle 4 and 5 to send message

expressive or meaningful, in the sense of distinct, processing level. The "A" in Figure 15.4 refers the reader to Figure 15.5.

We must carefully repeat that the examples of focusing-type information flows described here for the PhD history students, specifically the "bastardy arrears" example, is for only one feature of the information need frame. There are presumably several features that make up a complete information need frame. In Figure 15.5 we diagram the information flow from environmental textual stimulus leading to the production of a "feature," which we hypothesize is the beginning of the instantiation of a feature of the PhD student's information need frame. The "A" links this figure to Figure 15.4 which describes "single-feature" instantiation. In Figure 15.6, we diagrammed these features as separate Jigsaw Pieces, with each feature being a separate Piece.

15.3 Important Points of PhD History Students Study

We have utilized a study of 45 PhD history students (Cole, 1994a) to give evidentiary support to this book's theory of information need and how the theory works when the user is in a Focusing stage of performing a task. In the case of the study, the PhD students were researching and writing their doctoral dissertations. The emphasis in

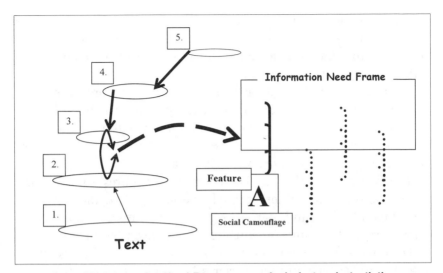

Figure 15.5   The Information Need Frame versus single-feature instantiation

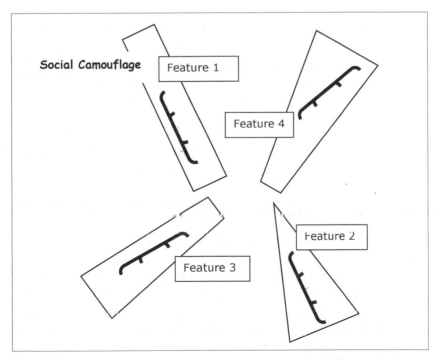

Figure 15.6   Example of how "social camouflage" fits into total Jigsaw as only one feature of many features

the study at the time of the study was the examination and analysis of major information processes of the PhD students, information processes that had a major effect on their task of researching and writing an original dissertation.

We have recoded the data from that study here into the more generic terminology of this book's theory of information need in order to illustrate how the theory works when the user is conducting an information search while in a Focusing phase. We will briefly summarize the important points of this illustration.

The first point is that the Focusing stage requires a preliminary stage of information gathering that is Pre-focus, where the user gathers general background material on the topic into a Picture. In the terminology of the information theory proposed by this book, the PhD students conducted Pre-focus information search by investigating evolving aspects of their dissertation topic. It is only from this general background reading that a focus for the task can emerge.

Focusing occurs when a PhD student recognizes an anomaly in the textual material he or she is reading. The background reading stored in the Picture allows the information user to recognize the anomalous point. At the very deepest level of the information need, the anomalous point indicates a change in the topic landscape-environment for the PhD student. The student then proceeds to adapt to this change by widening out the initiating anomalous environmental stimulus into this previously read contextual background material stored in the user's Picture area of memory.

The second point is that when the anomalous point widens out into the background reading in the Picture, the effect of the widening out in the Picture is to create a new expectation set. Because of the new expectation set, the PhD student was able to create questions to be answered or points to pursue further. The new expectation set, these new questions, directed the PhD students' subsequent information searching and seeking. In this way, the expectation set, operationalized here as the four-pronged symbol, shapes the end product, unless it is rejected by the user as a false route. The new end product resulting from the new expectation set, these new questions that needed answering, is the adaptation to the originally perceived anomaly in the textual environment. In other words, in more general terms for all users of information systems:

1. The user can adapt to anomaly or change in environmental landscape via background reading in the

Picture, but for more usual information need processes than the PhD student researching and writing a dissertation, the Picture can also include life experience. This was also evident in the quoted explanations of the PhD students we cite—that life experiences and common sense were part of the Picture.

2. The anomaly or change-stimulus widens out into the Picture creating a new expectation set, which determines subsequent information seeking/searching behavior.

Consequently, information need at its very deepest level is the recognition of anomalies in the environmental landscape, the creation of a new expectation set, and the process of information need at this deepest level is to effectuate the person's adaptation to the initiating anomaly in the environmental-textual landscape via new behavior (i.e., answering the new questions in the expectation set).

CHAPTER 16

Corroborating Research

The author and colleagues investigated the power of a new expectation set in a series of research studies from 2002–2010. Instead of PhD history students, we studied undergraduate history and psychology students who were assigned the task of researching and writing a social science essay. In a sense, these new subjects had smaller information processes and smaller Pictures than the PhD students. While the PhD students (in Britain) were required to hand in an original and substantive dissertation, the North American undergraduate history and psychology students in these new studies had a different task.

We defined the undergraduate students' task when they were researching and writing an essay required for their course work as putting their learning on display for the course instructor marking the essays. The best way to do this was to hand in a high impact essay-type assignment, based on finding and supporting an argument statement or thesis. This would prove to the course instructor that the students had engaged in critical thinking and had integrated their learning from course lectures and assigned and self-motivated voluntary readings.

In these studies, we utilized the same general interview schedule, whose purpose was to cause the students/subjects to think of information seeking/search in terms of questions they wanted an information system to answer. (For the full interview schedule, see appendix in Cole, Leide, Large, Beheshti, and Brooks, 2005, or Cole, Lin, Leide, Large, and Beheshti, 2007.) These new questions the undergraduate students came up with during the interview constituted their new expectation set.

The interview schedule asked the students/subjects to go through a series of cognitive steps in a 30–45 minute interview session. The students/subjects had to select one question from a set of four questions they wanted the information system to answer, which the interview schedule had them produce during the interview. As discussed in Part I of this book, the topic statement and information need of these students, who were interviewed when they were in a Pre-focus stage of researching and writing their undergraduate course essay, are completely different. We summarize the interview schedule here:

1. The student subject is asked to write down the topic of his or her essay paper and to identify the key concepts and key words from that topic statement.

2. The student is asked to visualize the concepts or key words from Step 1, and then label the visualizations (usually circles).

3. The student is asked, from the visualization in Step 2, to list the search terms.

4. The student is asked to visualize the search terms from Step 3 utilizing circles and connecting lines, varying the circles in size according to their importance to the final essay, and varying the distance apart of the circles according to how close the concepts represented by the circles will be in the essay.

5. The student is asked to write down four questions he or she would like answered by an information source, and then he or she is asked to rank the questions in order of importance to the essay.

6. The student is asked to come up with search terms for the question he or she ranked as most important.

The interview schedule was utilized again and again in this series of studies. The overall objective of the interview schedule was to facilitate the students/subjects, at the end of the interview, writing an effective information need statement that more accurately reflected their information need at that moment than terms taken from their original topic statement. The information need the students were asked to produce at the end of the interview was produced when they created a new expectation set and selected from the set the question that would most likely be in the final form of their course essay. No information searching was conducted during the 30–45 minute interview. However, because the research intervention took place early on in the term, when the students were predicted to be in a Pre-focus stage of information search, there was a 2-month lapse of time between the intervention and when the students handed in the finished essay for marking. The intervention, with the production of a new expectation set that accurately reflected their information need at the moment of the intervention, was intended to produce new, adaptive information search and seeking behavior during the time between the intervention and the hand-in of the finished essay. This was based on the notion of Minsky's (1975) frame theory, outlined in Part I of this book, of the expectation set for various features of a room, for example, or various features of an event such as a birthday party. Based on the person's previous experience with a room and birthday party, there would be an expectation set for each feature, with a default setting on the most likely alternative in the set.

The object of the interview schedule, the results of which will be summarized later, was to get the students/subjects to think of their essay in terms of a set of alternative questions, to rank the questions in terms of importance to the final form of their essay, and to then, in terms of this expectation set, derive search terms from a more exact representation of their real information need. The new expectation set—the four questions—asked the undergraduate students to think of their information need in terms of a goal state rather than a start state (i.e., the information need terms derived from the question were meant to facilitate the students obtaining information from the information system that would facilitate performance of their task of researching and writing a high impact, proof-of-learning undergraduate social science essay). For start-goal-state discussion, see Cole, Leide, Beheshti, Large, and Brooks, 2005; Spink and Cole, 2006.

The results we summarize here from these studies are based on quasi-experiment methodology with an intervention group or groups and a control group, with the dependent variable being a quantitative measure of essay researching/writing performance; for example, the mark received for the student essay by the course instructor. All studies summarized here had between 59–80 undergraduate students/subjects. All students/subjects were interviewed when they were in Stage 3, the Pre-focus or exploratory stage of Kuhlthau's (1993) ISP Model. The control group received a powerful intervention as required by the ethics committees of the institutions where these studies were carried out (the ethics committees required that the control group would not be placed at a disadvantage vis-à-vis the intervention group as the studies were carried out in real-life courses for actual course-required essays). None of the findings summarized here are statistically significant; thus, the summaries describe tendencies only. Based on the 30–45 minute interview schedule just summarized:

- Concept attainment took place, with the students/subjects increasing the number of concept terms over the course of the interview; they increased the number of relations between concept terms; they increased the sophistication of their essay style; and they created more vertical concept maps, which are more closely aligned with thesauri and other controlled vocabulary schemes created by domain experts (Cole, Leide, Large, Beheshti, and Brooks, 2005).

- The "four question" stage of the interview schedule, which required the subjects to probe deeply into their tacit knowledge to come up with four questions they wanted information from the database to answer, stimulated the students/subjects to shift dramatically out of low-impact to high-impact essay styles (from descriptive to Cause and Effect or Compare and Contrast essay types) (Cole, Leide, Beheshti, Large, and Brooks, 2005).

- Students/subjects given high-impact essay-type interventions based on Compare and Contrast and Cause and Effect devices, did not receive statistically significant higher marks from the course instructor than students/subjects in the control group. However, there was some indication that the devices based on high-impact essay styles, specifically the Cause and Effect essay type, may facilitate the undergraduate's interaction with information to the point where the student obtains a higher mark for the essay (Leide, Cole, Beheshti, Large, and Lin, 2007).

- It was found that the "four question" stage in the interview schedule caused the students/subjects' mental models to shift into a hierarchical position (from 24 percent to 35 percent), thus making them a better fit for effectively utilizing traditional thesauri (Cole, Lin, Leide, Large, and Beheshti, 2007).

The purpose of these just-cited studies was to begin to put into practice an information system specifically designed to produce an up-to-date expectation set for a specific group of information users, an expectation set that represented their deepest and best thinking on their essay topic at a specifically defined moment in time: when they were in the difficult, Pre-focus stage of performing their task of researching and writing an essay that put their learning on display, and in the best possible light, for the person who would evaluate their essay, the course instructor. The expectation set is an operational definition of the information need of these undergraduates in a Pre-focus stage of performing their task. With their up-to-date expectation set in hand, the students were then in the most advantageous position, to the best of their ability, to recognize and adapt to any new patterns in the information they were interacting with, such as new topic issues, solutions to information problems, and new avenues of thinking about their essay topic. Part III of the book is an illustrated application in storyboards of the theory and concepts described in this book.

Application of the Theory of Information Need to Information System Design

CHAPTER 17

Applying Information Need

Part III of the book illustrates the concepts and theory of Parts I and II to information system design for a user who is conducting an information search when he or she is in a Pre-focus stage of performing an information-based task. The system shown is designed to retrieve information items from a database, but it can do more than that: It is designed to facilitate the user's knowledge formation during the user's information accessing activity to facilitate instantiation of the user's deepest QI level of information need.

The system places the user's information need within a broad information science perspective: The user as a human making sense of life and thus making sense of his or her task, project, or assignment via information search. In addition, we take a broad, evolutionary psychology approach to the user's information need and how that information need works during information search by defining the user's task while conducting the search as an "adaptive problem" rather than only an information problem (Cosmides and Tooby, 1992, pp. 178, 180).

The goal of the information system when the user is in a Pre-focus, topic aspect investigation phase is to facilitate the user's actualization of his or her information need to the information system, which forms the user query to the system, via:

1. Showing the user his or her task during the information search, and integrating it into the search activity

2. Putting the user in a frame of mind to link the information access activity to his or her belief system

3. Metaphorically immersing the user in the neurology of information search (i.e., how the brain is hardwired to function during information pickup, information integration, and information support for positioning the

user vis-à-vis his or her task and his or her position in the world)

The third point is of particular concern because we believe it is the essence of what future information systems will look like, and more importantly, feel like to the user. They will seem natural, intuitive, like a second-nature information system. The conceptual exemplar for such a natural information system is Vannevar Bush's famous memex machine.

17.1 Vannevar Bush

In an influential article entitled "As We May Think," Vannevar Bush (1945) conceptualized an information retrieval (IR) machine, called the memex machine, which was designed to facilitate the way humans naturally think when they interact with their information-rich environment. He referred to this natural way of thinking as thinking by association. A stimulus in the environment, on the printed page, causes an association in our mind, a thought that we for some reason associate with the stimulus. And it is this associated reaction that directs our next impulse to seek information. Bush's memex machine was designed to "catch" this associated thought, allowing the memex user to instantaneously retrieve support information for it, and the next one, and the next one, and so on, creating a trail through the information store that duplicated and informationally supported the user's natural way of thinking about a topic.

Because Bush's IR machine was designed to facilitate the user's associative thinking by providing instantaneous informational support for it, the memex machine has been acknowledged as a model for the hypertext information environment of the internet (Houston and Harmon, 2007; Nelson, 1991; Nyce and Kahn, 1989); the internet supplies instantaneous information for a hyperlinked concept that is embedded in the text the user is reading (Nelson, 1991). For the memex machine's influence on information science, see Cronin, 2007; Smith, 1991.

Vannevar Bush's 1945 description of a memex machine conceptualizes a browsing-based vision of information search (via hypertext-search). Other internet-based examples of associationism in the design of current information search engines are Google's "wonder wheel" and for online public access catalogs (OPACs),

AquaBrowser's "word cloud" (for a further description, see Cole, Julien, and Leide, 2010).

17.2 Information Search: A Particular Case

The information systems of the near future could be designed for particular groups and particular tasks. The task for the particular information system we illustrate in Chapter 18 is researching and writing an undergraduate social science essay. As a teacher, one wants the undergraduate student to start a big essay assignment for the course near the beginning of the course so that the student will be able to put into practice in the essay the skills and reading the student has read during the full 3 months of the term. The point of the essay is to show the teacher that he or she has learned content and critical thinking skills during the course. The best way to do this is for the student to show in the essay that he or she has learned enough to develop a critical thinking faculty for the topic covered in the essay. The essay does this by requiring the student to form an idea or opinion about some topic in the course, referred to by its technical term as the essay's thesis or argument statement. The whole structure of the essay flows from the thesis, requiring the student to support the idea of the thesis with arguments combined with evidentiary support from the student's readings. This is frequently done by contrasting the student's thesis idea with some other view of the topic expressed in either the topic literature or in the course instructor's lectures. If the student can start the essay researching process right away early in the term instead of the week or night before it is due, the student will listen and do his or her readings more carefully, with the goal in mind of either developing or supporting the essay thesis idea. The essay becomes a learning integration device for the course, especially if it is started early in the term. Unfortunately, the student receives the course requirements the first class of the course, which includes the essay requirement due at the end of term, and he or she puts off the task until the week or even the night before it is due.

One of the reasons for student procrastination is a painful stage in the essay research process that has been well documented, particularly by Kuhlthau (1993). Kuhlthau created a six-stage model of the student seeking information for a school assignment task, called the ISP Model. Stage 1 is initiation when the student first receives the course requirements, including notification that an essay is expected at the end of the course; the essay component is usually 30–40 percent of the total course mark. Stage 2 is when the student selects the topic for the essay; this is a broad topic selection process dependent on, for example, a section of the course. A broad topic area in American history is the Vietnam War, so that is the essay topic. Stage 3 is when the student explores the topic area; this is a high-activity, information seeking period. The goal of Stage 3 is to identify and explore aspects of the topic so that the user can narrow in on a specific aspect of the topic in Stage 4, the focus formulation stage. The essay focus is a major step towards the formulation of the student's idea of a thesis for the essay. In Stage 5, the student collects evidentiary support for the idea of the thesis. And in Stage 6, the student prepares and hands in the essay for marking.

Stage 3 is the crucial information seeking stage for producing an essay, but it is a painful stage leading to an increase in uncertainty on the part of the student (Kuhlthau, 1993; Wilson, Ford, Foster, Ellis, and Spink, 2002). When the student achieves the focus for the essay in Stage 4, uncertainty goes down and continues to go down until the end of the task. Conquering the Stage 3 rise in uncertainty, which creatures a barrier to students, pushing so many to shut down because they cannot navigate through exploring information on their topic, is , therefore, the goal of the Astrolabe information system that follows in the next chapter.

CHAPTER 18

The Astrolabe: An Information System for Stage 3 Information Exploration

The Astrolabe is to be used in Stage 3 of the undergraduate student's task of researching and writing a social science essay. It is designed to manage the student's uncertainty/anxiety, and to, in effect, break the back of producing an essay by:

1. Showing the undergraduate the essay task format (Introduction, Section 1, Section 2, Section 3, and Conclusion with thesis statement)

2. Showing the student how to produce an idea/thesis for the essay

3. Positioning the student's Pre-focus mindset for integrative learning by asking the student to think in terms of seeking information for the production and support of an idea/thesis for the essay

4. Facilitating the instantiation of the user's deepest Q1 level of information need

The fourth point is of particular concern in the design of the Astrolabe information system. The instantiation of the user's information need is the central idea of the theory of information need proposed in Chapter 8, "A Theory of Information Need," and is illustrated in Figure 8.10. In the theory, the task of the user is considered an essential point in facilitating the user's instantiation of an information need. The task in the Astrolabe is the Compare and Contrast Essay, which is also the query formulation device utilized in the information system.

The positioning of the information system user vis-à-vis the topic and his or her position in the world, in an existential sense, is of primary importance in Chapter 8's theory of information. In the Astrolabe information system, we incorporate mythical elements in the user's quest for information—specifically astrology charts—and the atmosphere of the quest for information in the Astrolabe system (the lighthouses, the Topic Sea, placing the user as a navigator on a ship, etc.).Figures 18.1 through 18.18 illustrate the Astrolabe information system. It takes the student in storyboard fashion from the beginning to end of a single search session. The Astrolabe is an interface between the student and the information store (such as Google or some other database). The 15 illustrations were drawn by Michel Hellman.

Figure 18.1   The student is shown the overview of the Astrolabe, the Topic Sea.

Figure 18.2   The student is given her role and her ship.

Figure 18.3 The student stops at the main lighthouse for instructions, before entering the Topic Sea.

Figure 18.4 The student is metaphorically handed her navigation device, the Astrolabe (an actual device used widely in Medieval times by navigators and astronomers to determine latitude, longitude, and time of day).

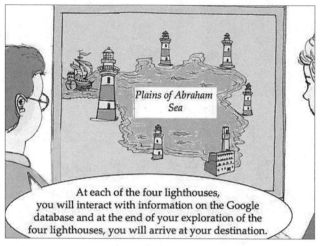

Figure 18.5 The student will stop at each of four lighthouses, where she will interact with the information database.

Figure 18.6 The student is asked to list of four questions she needs answered using information from the database.

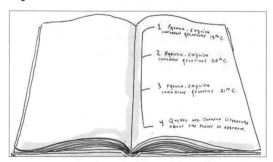

Figure 18.7 Here is an example of four questions taken from the topic "French-English relations in Canada."

Figure 18.8   Each of the four questions forms the query to the information store; each question is input at a separate lighthouse.

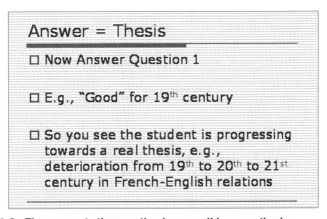

Figure 18.9   The answer to the question is a possible essay thesis.

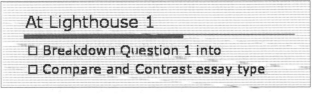

Figure 18.10   Compare and Contrast essay: The task device is introduced.

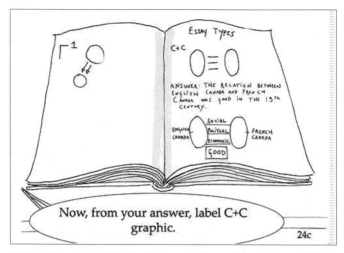

Figure 18.11   The student fills in the two circles and three lines, which form the keywords for the queries.

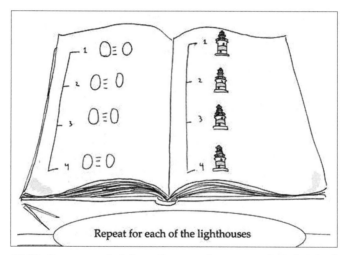

Figure 18.12   Four separate information searches are conducted at the four lighthouses. Each search is based on separate two circles/three lines query formulation devices.

Exploration

☐ Using the Astrolabe to find out where you are in your essay development vis-à-vis your destination (the final form of your essay)

Figure 18.13   Now the student utilizes the Astrolabe.

Figure 18.14   The student-navigator utilizes the Astrolabe by positioning him- or herself vis-à-vis the stars.

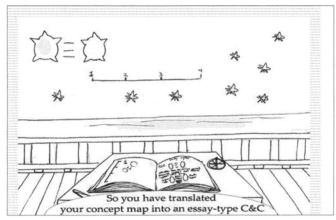

Figure 18.15   The Compare and Contrast Essay Device is placed amongst the stars. The student positions him- or herself vis-à-vis the essay topic and his or her position in the world.

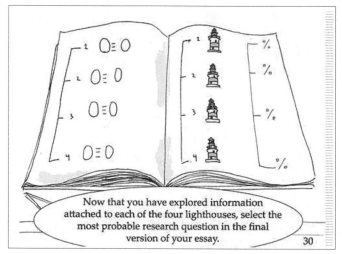

Figure 18.16   The student determines which information search/lighthouse is the most likely to be in the final version of the essay.

Figure 18.17   The third information search/lighthouse is 40 percent likely to be in the final version of the essay. Therefore, the student is 40 percent of the way to the destination. The student can return to the Astrolabe information system many times, and will gradually get to the destination, which equals 100 percent.

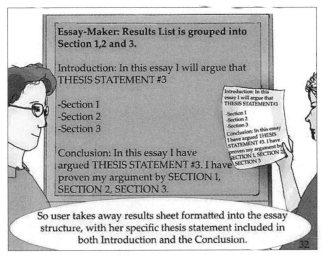

Figure 18.18 The student leaves the Astrolabe information system with the Introduction; Sections 1, 2, and 3 of the body of the essay; and the Conclusion labeled by the system. Sections 1, 2, and 3 are directly derived from the selected thesis statement. And Sections 1, 2, and 3 form the key terms in the student's query to the information store. The results list for that query is under each section.

Part **IV**

Conclusion

CHAPTER 19

The Arc of an Information Need

This book asks the questions: What is information need, and how does it work? The book addresses these questions from a wider perspective than is traditionally the case, by trying to get at its most fundamental level (i.e., information need as an adaptive human mechanism that drives humans to seek out, recognize, and then adapt to changes in their social and physical environments). We believe this broad, holistic perspective, which links information search to knowledge formation, may facilitate the information system designer's task of developing systems that enable the greatest number of people to ably access information from an information system, using found information to discern and benefit their position in their work and everyday lives.

Here we summarize the book with the illustrative diagrams utilized throughout Parts I and II that visualize the mechanisms underlying information need. Part II emphasizes how information need works when the user is in a Pre-focus stage of performing an information-based task, and when the user is in a Focusing stage of performing an information-based task. In this summary, in order to indicate the complete arc of information search stages, we analyze how an information need works during an information search when the user is performing an information-based task. The summary is contained in Figures 19.1, 19.2, and 19.3, which together take the reader through a complete Pre-focus, Focusing, and Post-focus cycle.

Figure 19.1 begins with the user in a Pre-focus stage of performing an information-based task. In this stage, the user does not know the topic, its problems, issues, controversies, and so on, and therefore cannot form an opinion or make judgments on the material. This includes making relevance judgments regarding the system output in the results list. By definition, the environmental stimuli coming at this user from the results list is unfamiliar and unexpected. Even though the user has no opinion either way about the results list, from life experience and previous reading and knowledge, a certain amount of information nonetheless begins to register in the user's perceptual system. Gradually, this user builds up a Picture of his or her topic, illustrated in Figure 19.1(a), which is made up of general reading on the topic. This is an important stage because it prepares the perceptual system for other encounters with the same pattern of information, resulting in the user being able to perceive patterns in subsequently encountered material. These patterns become aspects of the user's search topic, from which, eventually, emerges a sort of aspect map of the topic, shown in Figure 19.1(b). The edges of the map are vague, not clearly defined, so it is still difficult for the user to identify information that belongs to one "aspect" part of the map or another. The user is still discriminating and identifying aspect categories.

Aspects can be defined as issues, problems, or a perspective in the topic area that the user obtains from related readings. The aspect map eventually becomes more distinct as the user becomes more certain of the issues, problems, and so on, in the topic area through iterations with similar patterns in the information, so the map morphs into Jigsaw Pieces, illustrated in Figure 19.1(c). In Figure 19.1(a) through (c) we are in the user's Pre-focus stage of performing the task, which is equivalent to Kuhlthau's (1993) Stage 3 of her six-stage IPS Model, where the user is still exploring the topic area.

We have long wondered what differentiates Kuhlthau's third and fourth stage, given that focus formation occurs sometime in Stage 4, but not at the beginning of this stage. The material provided in this book sheds some light on this question. We hypothesize that at the end of Stage 3 the user has developed a notion of the aspects of the topic; but at the beginning of Stage 4 these notions turn into firm categories. As discussed in Part I of the book, categorization is the identification of the central and invariant features of the aspect. Stage 4 begins when one or more of the aspects develop feature characteristics of the category. A category can be an abstract idea. The user, for example, says: Oh, this information is part of the system versus user distinction in information system design. The user is now crossed over into a Focusing stage of performing the information-based task.

Figure 19.2(d) through (f) summarizes the user in a Focusing stage of performing an information-based task. One or more of the aspects the user is investigating develops feature characteristics of the aspect category, illustrated in Figure 19.2(d). The features form subcategories at this stage. As discussed in Part I, the categorization process

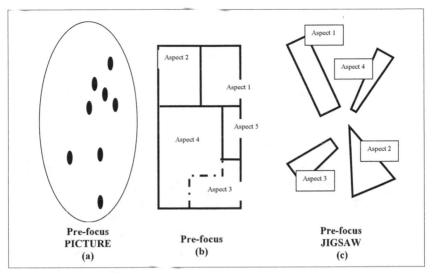

Figure 19.1   User in Pre-focus stage (a) through (c)

involves identifying the salient and invariant features of the category. We operationally define the aspect-to-feature change as the development of an expectation set. The alternatives in the expectation set represent these salient and invariant features of the subcategory or feature, represented in Figure 19.2(e) by the four-pronged symbol.

For the Figure 19.2(e) expectation set, we illustrate, with an example from the information need issues raised in this book, expectation sets for features of the category "information need" (not all expectation sets conform to the four alternatives in the four-pronged symbol):

Feature 1: Information need is evolving versus non-evolving.

- Information need evolves over stages of task performance.

- Information need does not evolve over stages of task performance.

- Information need appears to evolve, manifesting itself to the user as evolving.

- An information-based task is made up of many distinct and separate information needs, one for each time a person seeks information.

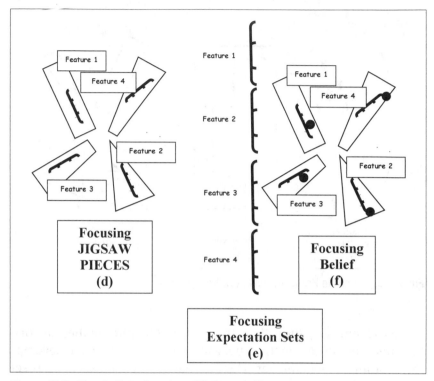

Figure 19.2 User in Focusing stage (d) through (f)

Feature 2: Information need is command versus question.

- User's query to information system represents a command to the system.

- User's query to information system represents a question to the system.

- User's query to information system can be both command and question.

Feature 3: Information need is associated with what kind of information?

- Information is a "thing" (see Buckland, 1991).

- Information is a "process" (Buckland, 1991).

- Information is "knowledge" (Buckland, 1991).

Feature 4: Information need is system- versus user-defined.

- Information need should be defined as a system-oriented concept.

- Information need should be defined as a user-oriented concept.

- Information need should somehow be defined as both a system-oriented and user-oriented concept.

In Figure 19.2(f), we indicate the "belief" alternative for each feature expectation set with a black dot attached to one of the alternatives in the set. The black dot indicates the user's belief for this alternative over all other alternatives in the set, over some threshold, say, 50 percent. This is at the "primitive" level of belief as defined by Rokeach (1960, p. 40), as the user has progressed to the point where he or she can say: I believe "X" to be most probably true from among the alternatives in the expectation set.

Figure 19.3 is speculative, indicating future directions for research. The situation of the user has developed from the Focusing stage illustrated in Figure 19.2. With the user's belief, the user has now allied and therefore immersed him- or herself in a point of view about an issue, problem, or controversy in the topic area, specifically for the feature of the category for which he or she has now taken sides. We hypothesize that the generative apparatus of the user's neurological system kicks in, represented in Figure 19.3(g) by four levels of linked Association Wheels. The user's belief or opinion on an issue or topic-related problem or controversy is supported in the information literature by a theoretical system or a conceptual framework. The user assumes this theoretical system/conceptual framework support for the belief. This positions the user inside a theoretical framework made up of associated concepts, propositions, and relations. When the category feature belief becomes linked to the user's higher belief system, it then implicates the user's position in a social or work environment, and his or her position in the world on an existential level; at this point, we hypothesize that the user's information need becomes fully instantiated down to its deepest Q1 level, illustrated in 19.3(h). The final phase of Focusing, where we hypothesize that the focus is achieved, is the user's overall view, opinion, or thesis about the topic occurring as a result of the interaction of the various features, again operationalized as Association Wheels consisting of associated concepts and relations, illustrated in 19.3(i). When this interaction of the features or Jigsaw Pieces occurs, we hypothesize that the user's information need instantiates in a task focus. We illustrate the focus with the thesis of this book, illustrated in 19.3(j).

The thesis of this book and the theory of information need the book proposes is that information need is made up of levels, and is not made up of phases. Taylor (1968) has been misinterpreted to mean a phase-approach or an evolution- or shifting-approach to information need. Information need, on the other hand, may manifest itself to the user as evolving and constantly shifting and changing. But the central thesis of this book is that the underlying information need in fact does not instantiate fully until the user achieves focus.

Only the levels perspective on information need will achieve the linkage of knowledge formation and information access in information

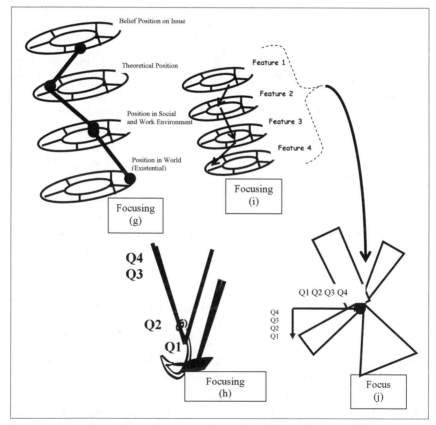

Figure 19.3 Final stages of Focusing (g) to (j), and instantiation of full information need to deepest Q1 level

system design that we believe necessary to overcome the information overload issues we all face in a Pre-focus stage of performing an
information-based task, and the information literacy issues the
informationally disadvantaged in our society face because they see
information, information use, critical thinking, and the information
age as strange abominations that only others can use.

References

Alexander, R. D. (1990). How did humans evolve? Reflections on the uniquely unique species. University of Michigan Museum of Zoology, Special Publications (Vol. 1, pp. 1–38). Accessed September 30, 2011, from insects.ummz.lsa.umich.edu/pdfs/Alexander1990.pdf.

Allen, T. J. (1966). The differential performance of information channels in the transfer of technology. Massachusetts Institute of Technology, Cambridge, MA, June 1966, 28 p (Alfred P. Sloan School of Management. Working Paper, no. 196–66). Accessed September 30, 2011, from www.archive.org/details/differentialperf00alle.

Allen, T. J (1969). Information needs and uses. In C. A. Cuadra (Ed.), *Annual Review of Information Science and Technology*, 4, 3–29.

Allen, T. J., & Frischmuth, D. S. (1968). A model for the description and evaluation of technical problem solving. Cambridge, MA: Working Paper, no. 316–68. Alfred P. Sloan School of Management, Massachusetts Institute of Technology, March 1968.

Allen, T. J., Gerstenfeld, A., & Gerstberger, P. G. (1968). The problem of internal consulting in an R&D laboratory. Working Paper, no. 319–68. Alfred P. Sloan School of Management. Massachusetts Institute of Technology, Cambridge, MA. Accessed September 30, 2011, from dspace.mit.edu/bitstream/handle/1721.1/48828/problemofinterna00alle.pdf?sequence=1.

Anderson, J. R., & Bower, G. H. (1973). *Human Associative Memory*. Washington, D.C.: V. H. Winston & Sons.

Arbib, M. A. (1983). Cognitive science: The view from brain theory. In F. Machlup & U. Mansfield (Eds.), *The Study of Information: Interdisciplinary Messages* (pp. 81–91). New York: John Wiley & Sons.

Baddeley, A. D. (2001). Is working memory still working? *American Psychologist*, 56, 851–864.

Baker, N. R., Siegmann, J., & Rubenstein, A. H. (1967). The effects of perceived needs and means on the generation of ideas for industrial research development projects. IEEE Transactions on Engineering Management, EM-14(4), 156–163.

Baker, S. L., & Lancaster, F. W. (1991). *The Measurement and Evaluation of Library Services.* Arlington, VA: Information Resources Press.

Barsalou, L. W. (1983). Ad-hoc categories. *Memory and Cognition,* 11, 211–227.

Bartlett, F. C. (1932). *Remembering.* Cambridge, U.K.: Cambridge University Press.

Bates, M. J. (1989). The design of browsing and berrypicking techniques for the online search interface. *Online Review,* 13(5), 407–424.

Bates, M. J. (1998). Indexing and access for digital libraries and the Internet: Human, database, and domain factors. *Journal of the American Society for Information Science,* 49(13), 1185–1205.

Bawden, D. (1986). Information systems and the simulation of creativity. *Journal of Information Science,* 12(5), 203–216.

Belkin, N. J. (1980). Anomalous States of Knowledge as a basis for information retrieval. *Canadian Journal of Information Science,* 5, 133–143.

Belkin, N. J., Oddy, R. N., & Brooks, H. M. (1982a). ASK for information retrieval, Part I: Background and theory. *Journal of Documentation,* 38(2), 61–71.

Belkin, N. J., Oddy, R. N., & Brooks, H. M. (1982b). ASK for information retrieval, Part II: Results of a design study. *Journal of Documentation,* 38(3), 145–164.

Belkin, N. J., & Vickery, A. (1985). *Interaction in Information Systems: A Review of Research from Document Retrieval to Knowledge-based Systems.* Boston Spa, U.K.: British Library.

Bernal, J. D. (1948). Preliminary analysis of pilot questionnaire on the use of scientific literature. In *Royal Society Report on the Royal Society Scientific Information Conference* (pp. 589–637). London: Royal Society.

Bernal, J. D. (1957). The supply of information to the scientist: Some problems of the present day. *Journal of Documentation,* 13(4), 195–208.

Berul, L. H. (1969). Document retrieval. In C. A. Cuadra (Ed.), *Annual Review of Information Science and Technology,* 4, 203–227.

Bialystok, E., & Olson, D. R. (1987). Spatial categories: The perception and conceptualization of spatial relations. In S. Harnad (Ed.), *Categorical Perception: The Groundwork of Cognition* (pp. 511–531). Cambridge, U.K.: Cambridge University Press.

Borgman, C. L. (2000). *From Gutenberg to the Global Information Infrastructure.* Cambridge, MA: The MIT Press.

Boudon, R. (1991). Review: What middle-range theories are. *Contemporary Sociology,* 20(4), 519–522.

Brittain, J. M. (1970). *Information and Its Users: A Review with Special Reference to the Social Sciences.* New York: Wiley.

Brookes, B. C. (1980). The foundations of information science, Part I: Philosophical aspects. *Journal of Information Science,* 2, 125–133.

Bruner, J. S. (1951). Personality dynamics and the process of perceiving. In R. R. Blake & G. V. Ramsey (Eds.), *Perception: An Approach to Personality* (pp. 121–147). New York: The Ronald Press Company.

Bruner, J.S. (1957). On perceptual readiness. *Psychological Review,* 64, 123–152.

Bruner, J. S., Goodnow, J. J., & Austin, G. A. (1956). *A Study of Thinking.* New York: Wiley.

Buckland, M. K. (1991). Information as thing. *Journal of the American Society for Information Science,* 42(5), 351–360.

Buckland, M. K. (1992). Emanuel Goldberg, electronic document retrieval, and Vannevar Bush's Memex. *Journal of the American Society for Information Science,* 43(4), 284–294.

Buckley, W. (1983). Signals, meaning, and control in social systems. In F. Machlup & U. Mansfield (Eds.), *Study of Information: Interdisciplinary Messages* (pp. 601–606). New York: John Wiley & Sons.

Burke, C. (1992). A practical view of memex: The career of the rapid selector. In J. M. Nyce & P. Kahn (Eds.), *From Memex to Hypertext: Vannevar Bush and the Mind's Machine* (pp. 145–164). Boston: Academic Press.

Burke, C. B., & Buckland, M. K. (1994). *Information and Secrecy: Vannevar Bush, Ultra and the Other Memex.* Metuchen, NJ: Scarecrow Press.

Bush, V. (1945). As we may think. *Atlantic Monthly,* 176(1), 101–108.

Cao, J., Liang, J., & Lam, J. (2004). Exponential stability of high-order bidirectional associative memory neural networks with time delays. *Physica D: Nonlinear Phenomena,* 199(3–4), 425–436.

Carnap, R. (1950). *Logical Foundations of Probability*. Chicago: University of Chicago Press.

Case, D. O. (2002). *Looking for Information: A Survey of Research on Information Seeking, Needs, and Behavior*. Amsterdam: Academic Press.

Case, D. O. (2007). *Looking for Information: A Survey of Research on Information Seeking, Needs, and Behavior*. London: Academic Press.

Cauvin, J. (2000). *The Birth of the Gods and the Origins of Agriculture*. Cambridge, MA: Cambridge University Press.

Chatman, E. A. (1996). The impoverished life-world of outsiders. *Journal of the American Society for Information Science*, 47(3), 193–206.

Chomsky, N. (1980). Rules and representations. *Behavioral and Brain Sciences*, 3, 1–61.

Cole, C. (1994a). Information as modification of knowledge structure: How Ph.D. history students become informed. Ph.D. thesis in partial fulfillment of a Ph.D. degree, Department of Information Studies, University of Sheffield, UK.

Cole, C. (1994b). Operationalizing the notion of information as a subjective construct. *Journal of the American Society for Information Science*, 45(7), 465–476.

Cole, C. (1998). Information acquisition in history Ph.D. students: Inferencing and the formation of knowledge structures. *Library Quarterly*, 68(1), 33–54.

Cole, C. (2000a). Inducing expertise in history doctoral students via enabling information retrieval design. *Library Quarterly*, 70(1), 86–109.

Cole, C. (2000b). Name collection by Ph.D. history students: Inducing expertise. *Journal of the American Society for Information Science*, 51(5), 444–455.

Cole, C. (2008). A socio-cognitive framework for designing interactive IR systems: Lessons from the Neanderthals. *Information Processing & Management*, 44, 1784–1793.

Cole, C. (2011). A theory of information need for IR that connects information to knowledge. *Journal of the American Society for Information Science and Technology*, 62(7), 1216–1231.

Cole, C., Cantero, P., & Ungar, A. (2000). The development of a diagnostic-prescriptive tool for undergraduates seeking information for a social science/humanities assignment, Part III: Enabling devices. *Information Processing and Management*, 36(3), 481–500.

Cole, C., Julien, C. A., & Leide, J. E. (2010). An associative index model for hypertext Internet search based on Vannevar Bush's Memex machine: An exploratory case study. *Information Research*, 15(3), paper 435. Accessed September 30, 2011, from www.informationr.net/ir/15-3/paper435.html.

Cole, C., & Kuhlthau, C. (2000). Information and information seeking of novice versus expert lawyers: How experts add value. *New Review of Information Behaviour Research*, 1, 103–115.

Cole, C., Leide, J. E., Beheshti, J., Large, A., & Brooks, M. (2005). Investigating the ASK hypothesis in a real-life problem situation: A study of history and psychology undergraduates seeking information for a course essay. *Journal of the American Society for Information Science and Technology*, 56(14), 1544–1554.

Cole, C., Leide, J. E., Large, A., Beheshti, J., & Brooks, M. (2005). Putting it together online: Information need identification for the domain novice user. *Journal of the American Society for Information Science and Technology*, 56(7), 684–694.

Cole, C., Lin, Y., Leide, J. E., Large, A., & Beheshti, J. (2007). A classification of mental models of undergraduates seeking information for a course essay in history and psychology: Preliminary investigations into aligning their mental models with online thesauri. *Journal of the American Society for Information Science and Technology*, 58(13), 2092–2104.

Collins, A. M., & Quillian, M. R. (1969). Retrieval time from semantic memory. *Journal of Verbal Learning and Verbal Behavior*, 8, 240–247.

Conway, A. R. A., Cowan, N., & Bunting, M. F. (2001). The cocktail party phenomenon revisited: The importance of working memory capacity. *Psychonomic Bulletin & Review*, 8, 331–335.

Cosmides, L., & Tooby, J. (1987). From evolution to behavior: Evolutionary psychology as the missing link. In J. Dupre (Ed.), *The Latest on the Best: Essays on Evolution and Optimality* (pp. 227–306). Cambridge, MA: MIT Press.

Cosmides, L., & Tooby, J. (1992). Cognitive adaptations for social exchange. In J. Barkow, L. Cosmides, & J. Tooby (Eds.), *The Adapted*

Mind: Evolutionary Psychology and the Generation of Culture (pp. 163–228). New York: Oxford University Press.

Crane, D. (1971). Information needs and uses. In C. A. Cuadra (Ed.), *Annual Review of Information Science and Technology*, 6, 3–40.

Cronin, B. (2007). Introduction. *Annual Review of Information Science and Technology*, 41, vii–x.

Cutter, C. A. (1904). *Rules for a Dictionary Catalog.* (4th. ed.). Washington, D.C.: U.S. Government Printing Office. Accessed September 30, 2011, from www.digital.library.unt.edu/ark:/67531/metadc1048/m1/1. (Archived by WebCite at www.webcitation.org/ 5s66uVQnF.)

Dannatt, R. J. (1967). Books, information and research: Libraries for technological universities. *Minerva*, 5(2), 209–226.

Dervin, B. (1992). From the mind's eye of the user: The sense-making qualitative-quantitative methodology. In J. Glazier & R. Powell (Eds.), *Qualitative Research in Information Management* (pp. 61–84). Englewood, CO: Libraries Unlimited.

Dervin, B. (1999). On studying information seeking methodologically: The implications of connecting metatheory to method. *Information Processing & Management*, 35, 727–750.

Dervin, B. (2003a). Chaos, order, and sense-making: A proposed theory for information design. In B. Dervin, L. Foreman-Wernet, & E. Lauterbach (Eds.), *Sense-making Methodology Reader: Selected Writings of Brenda Dervin* (pp. 325–340). Cresskill, NJ: Hampton Press Inc.

Dervin, B. (2003b). From the mind's eye of the user: The sense-making qualitative-quantitative methodology. In B. Dervin, L. Foreman-Wernet, & E. Lauterbach (Eds.), *Sense-making Methodology Reader: Selected Writings of Brenda Dervin* (pp. 269–292). Cresskill, NJ: Hampton Press Inc.

Dervin, B., Jacobson, T. L., & Nilan, M. S. (1982). Measuring aspects of information seeking: A test of quantitative/qualitative methodology. In M. Burgoon (Ed.), *Communication Yearbook*, 6 (pp. 419–444). Beverly Hills, CA: Sage.

Dervin, B., & Nilan, M. (1986). Information needs and uses. *Annual Review of Information Science and Technology*, 21, 3–33.

Donald, M. (1991). *Origins of the Modern Mind: Three Stages in the Evolution of Culture and Cognition*. Cambridge, MA: Harvard University Press.

Dubrovsky, B. (2002). Evolutionary psychiatry. Adaptationist and nonadaptationist conceptualizations. *Progress in Neuro-Psychopharmacology and Biological Psychiatry*, 26(1), 1–19.

Dumais, S., & Belkin, N. J. (2005). The TREC interactive tracks: Putting the user into search. In E. M. Voorhees & D. K. Harman (Eds.), *TREC: Experiment and Evaluation in Information Retrieval* (pp. 123–152). Cambridge, MA: MIT Press.

Duncan, J., Emslie, H., Williams, P., Johnson, R., & Freer, C. (1996). Intelligence and the frontal lobe: The organization of goal-directed behavior. *Cognitive Psychology*, 30, 257–303.

Dwyer, C. M., Gossen, E. A., & Martin, L. M. (1991). Known-item search failure in an OPAC. *RQ*, 31(2), 228–236.

Eigen, M. (2007). Letters to the Editor. The bright side of human nature. *New York Times* (p. A22). (February 21, 2007).

Ellis, D., Wilson, T. D., Ford, N., Lam, H. M., Burton, R., & Spink, A. (2002). Information seeking and mediated searching, Part 5: User-intermediary interaction. *Journal of the American Society for Information Science and Technology*, 53(11), 883–893.

Engelbert, H. (1968). In German. Probleme der Erforschung des Informationsbedorfs der Gesellschaftswissenschaften. *ZIID Zeitschrift*, 15(6), 243–248.

Fodor, J. A. (1985). Précis of "The modularity of mind." *Behavioral and Brain Sciences*, 8, 1–42.

Ford, N. (2004). Creativity and convergence in information science research: The roles of objectivity and subjectivity, constraint, and control. *Journal of the American Society for Information Science and Technology*, 55(13), 1169–1182.

Ford, N., Wilson, T. D., Foster, A., Ellis, D., & Spink, A. (2002). Information seeking and mediated searching, Part 4: Cognitive styles and individual differences. *Journal of the American Society for Information Science and Technology*, 53(9), 728–735.

Frischmuth, D. S., & Allen, T. J. (1968). A model for the description and evaluation of technical problem solving. Working Paper. Alfred P. Sloan School of Management. Massachusetts Institute of Technology, Cambridge, Massachusetts. Accessed September 30, 2011, from dspace.mit.edu/bitstream/handle/1721.1/48450/modelfordescript00fris.pdf?sequence=1.

Glaser, B. G., & Strauss, A. L. (1967). *The Discovery of Grounded Theory: Strategies for Qualitative Research.* New Brunswick, NJ: Aldine Publishing Company.

Gobet, F., & Charness, N. (2006). Expertise in chess. In K. A. Ericsson, N. Charness, P. J. Feltovich, & R. R. Hoffman (Eds.), *Cambridge Handbook of Expertise and Expert Performance* (pp. 523–538). Cambridge, U.K.: Cambridge University Press.

Harmon, G. (1970). Information need transformation during inquiry: A reinterpretation of user relevance. In *Proceedings of the American Society for Information Science Annual Meeting* (33rd, Philadelphia, October 11–15, 1970), vol. 7, 41–43.

Harnad, S. (1987a). Category induction and representation. In S. Harnad (Ed.), *Categorical Perception: The Groundwork of Cognition* (pp. 535–565). Cambridge, U.K.: Cambridge University Press.

Harnad, S. (1987b). Psychophysical and cognitive aspects of categorical perception: A critical overview. In S. Harnad (Ed.), *Categorical Perception: The Groundwork of Cognition* (pp. 1–25). Cambridge, U.K.: Cambridge University Press.

Hearst, M. A. (1999). User interfaces and visualization. In B. Y. Ricardo & R. N. Berthier (Eds.), *Modern Information Retrieval* (pp. 257–323). New York: ACM Press.

Herner, S., & Herner, M. (1967). Information needs and uses in science and technology. In C. A. Cuadra (Ed.), *Annual Review of Information Science and Technology*, 2, 1–34.

Hillman, D. J. (1968). Negotiation of inquiries in an on-line retrieval system. *Information Storage and Retrieval*, 4(2), 219–238.

Hirtle, S. C., & Heidorn, P. B. (1993). The structure of cognitive maps: Representations and processes. In T. Garling & R. G. Golledge (Eds.), *Behavior and Environment: Psychological and Geographical Approaches* (pp. 170–192). Amsterdam: North-Holland.

Hjørland, B. (2010). The foundation of the concept of relevance. *Journal of the American Society for Information Science and Technology*, 61(2), 217–237.

Houston, R. D., & Harmon, G. (2007). Vannevar Bush and memex. *Annual Review of Information Science and Technology*, 41, 55–92.

Jansen, B. J., & Rieh, S. Y. (2010). The seventeen theoretical constructs of information search and information retrieval. *Journal of the*

American Society for Information Science and Technology, 61(8), 1517–1534.

Kane, M. J., Bleckley, M. K., Conway, A. R. A., & Engle, R. W. (2001). A controlled-attention view of working-memory capacity. *Journal of Experimental Psychology: General*, 130(2), 169–183.

Kane, M. J., & Engle, R. W. (2002). The role of prefrontal cortex in working-memory capacity, executive attention, and general fluid intelligence: An individual-differences perspective. *Psychonomic Bulletin & Review*, 9, 637–671.

Kaplan, S. (1992). Environmental preference in a knowledge-seeking, knowledge-using organism. In J. H. Barkow, L. Cosmides, & J. Tooby (Eds.), *The Adapted Mind: Evolutionary Psychology and the Generation of Culture* (pp. 581–598). New York: Oxford University Press.

Kendler, H. H., & Kendler, T. S. (1962). Vertical and horizontal processes in problem solving. *Psychological Review*, 69(1), 1–16.

Kochen, M. (1969). Stability in the growth of knowledge. *American Documentation*, 20(3), 186–197.

Kuhlthau, C. C. (1993). *Seeking Meaning: A Process Approach to Library and Information Services*. Norwood, NJ: Ablex Publishing.

Kunz, W., Rittel, H. W. J., & Schwuchow, W. (1977). *Methods of Analysis and Evaluation of Information Needs: A Critical Review*. Munich: Verlag Dokumentation.

Lancaster, F. W., & Joncich, M. J. (1977). *The Measurement and Evaluation of Library Services*. Washington, D.C.: Information Resources Press.

Langlois, R. N. (1983). Systems theory, knowledge, and the social sciences. In F. Machlup & U. Mansfield (Eds.), *The Study of Information: Interdisciplinary Messages* (pp. 493–600). New York: John Wiley & Sons.

Lee, J. H., Renear, A., & Smith, L. C. (2006). Known-item search: Variations on a concept. In A. Grove (Ed.), *Proceedings of the 69th Annual Meeting of the American Society for Information Science and Technology (ASIST)*, 43(1), 1–17.

Leide, J. E., Cole, C., Beheshti, J., Large, A., & Lin, Y. (2007). Task-based IR: Essay-types as query formulation devices for undergraduates researching a history essay. *Journal of the American Society for Information Science and Technology*, 58(9), 1227–1241.

Lewis, D. W. (1987). Research on the use of online catalogs and its implications for library practice. *Journal of Academic Librarianship,* 13(3), 152–156.

Lewis-Williams, D., & Pearce, D. (2005). *Inside the Neolithic Mind: Consciousness, Cosmos and the Realm of the Gods.* New York: Thames & Hudson.

Lin, N., & Garvey, W. D. (1972). Information needs and uses. In C. A. Cuadra (Ed.), *Annual Review of Information Science and Technology,* 7, 5–38.

Line, M. B. (1971). The information uses and needs of social scientists: An overview of INFROSS. *Aslib Proceedings,* 23(8), 412–434.

Lipetz, B. A. (1970). Information needs and uses. In C. A. Cuadra (Ed.), *Annual Review of Information Science and Technology,* 5, 3–28.

MacKay, D. M. (1953/1955). Operational aspects of some fundamental concepts of human communication. *Synthese,* 9(3/5), 182–198.

MacKay, D. M. (1969). *Information, Mechanism and Meaning.* Boston: MIT Press.

MacKay, D. M. (1983). The wider scope of information theory. In F. Machlup & U. Mansfield (Eds.), *The Study of Information: Interdisciplinary Messages* (pp. 485–492). New York: John Wiley & Sons.

Madden, A. D. (2004). Evolution and information. *Journal of Documentation,* 60(1), 9–23.

Martín-Loeches, M. (2006). On the uniqueness of humankind: Is language working memory the final piece that made us human? *Journal of Human Evolution,* 50, 226–229.

Matthews, J. R., Lawrence, G. S., Ferguson, D. K., & Council on Library Resources. (1983). *Using Online Catalogs.* New York: Neal-Schuman.

Meadow, C. T., Boyce, B. R., Kraft, D. H., & Barry, C. (2007). *Text Information Retrieval Systems.* 3rd edition. San Diego: Academic Press.

Medin, D. L., & Rips, L. J. (2005). Concepts and categories: Memory, meaning, and metaphysics. In K. J. Holyoak & R. G. Morrison (Eds.), *Cambridge Handbook of Thinking and Reasoning* (pp. 37–72). New York: Cambridge University Press.

Menzel, H. (1966). Information needs and uses in science and technology. In C. A. Cuadra (Ed.), *Annual Review of Information Science and Technology,* 1, 41–69.

Menzel, H. (1967). Can science information needs be ascertained empirically? In L. Thayer (Ed.), *Communications: Concepts and Perspectives* (pp. 279–295). Washington, D.C.: Spartan Books.

Menzel, H. (1968). Informal communication in science: Its advantages and its formal analogues. In E. B. Montgomery (Ed.), *Foundations of Access to Knowledge* (pp. 153–163). Syracuse, NY: Syracuse University Press.

Miller, G. A. (1983a). Information theory in psychology. In F. Machlup & U. Mansfield (Eds.), *Study of Information: Interdisciplinary Messages* (pp. 493–496). New York: John Wiley & Sons.

Miller, G. A. (1983b). Informavores. In F. Machlup & U. Mansfield (Eds.), *Study of Information: Interdisciplinary Messages* (pp. 111–113). New York: John Wiley & Sons.

Minsky, M. (1975). A framework for representing knowledge. In P. H. Winston (Ed.), *Psychology of Computer Vision* (pp. 211–277). New York: McGraw-Hill.

Minsky, M. (1980). A framework for representing knowledge. In D. Meting (Ed.), *Frame Conceptions and Text Understanding* (pp. 1–25). Berlin: Walter de Gruyter.

Mithin, S. (1996). *The Prehistory of the Mind: The Cognitive Origins of Art, Religions and Science*. London: Thames and Hudson.

Nelson, T. H. (1991). As we will think. In J. M. Nyce & P. Kahn (Eds.), *From Memex to Hypertext. Vannevar Bush and the Mind's Machine* (pp. 245–260). Boston: Academic Press.

Nicolaisen, J. (2009). Compromised need and the label effect: An examination of claims and evidence. *Journal of the American Society for Information Science and Technology*, 60(10), 2004–2009.

Nyce, J. M., & Kahn, P. (1989). Innovation, pragmaticism, and technological continuity: Vannevar Bush's memex. *Journal of the American Society for Information Science*, 40(3), 214–220.

O'Conner, J. (1968). Some questions concerning information need. *American Documentation*, 19(2), 200–203.

Otlet, P. (1934). *Traité de documentation*. Brussels: Éditions mundaneum. Reprinted Liège, Belgium: Centre de lecture publique de la communauté française. 1989.

Oxford Dictionary of Current English (1984). Oxford, U.K.: Oxford University Press.

Paisley, W. J. (1968). Information needs and uses. In C. A. Cuadra (Ed.), *Annual Review of Information Science and Technology*, 3, 1–30.

Parker, E. B., Lingwood, D. A., & Paisley, W. J. (1968). Communication and research productivity in an interdisciplinary behavioral science research area. Institute for Communication Research, Stanford University, Stanford, California.

Piaget, J. (1950). *The Psychology of Intelligence*. London: Routledge and Kegan Paul.

Pirolli, P. (2007). *Information Foraging Theory: Adaptive Interaction with Information*. Oxford: Oxford University Press.

Plotkin, H. (2004). *Evolutionary Thought in Psychology: A Brief History*. Malden, MA: Blackwell.

Popper, K. (1975). *Objective Knowledge: An Evolutionary Approach*. Oxford: Clarendon Press.

Raaijmakers, J. G. W., & Shiffrin, R. M. (1981). Search of associative memory. *Psychological Review*, 88(2), 93–134.

Ratcliff, R. (1978). A theory of memory retrieval. *Psychological Review*, 85(2), 59–108.

Rees, A. M. (1963). Information needs and patterns of usage. In *Western Reserve University, School of Library Science, Center for Documentation and Communication Research. Information Retrieval in Action* (pp. 17–23). Cleveland, OH: Western Reserve University Press.

Rees, A. M., & Schultz, D. G. (1967). A field experimental approach to the study of relevance assessments in relation to document searching. Final report (July 1, 1965–June 30, 1967). Center for Documentation and Communication Research, Case Western Reserve University, Cleveland, Ohio, 1967.

Rokeach, M. (1960). *The Open and Closed Mind: Investigations into the Nature of Belief Systems and Personality Systems*. New York: Basic Books.

Rosch, E. (1973). On the internal structure of perceptual and semantic categories. In T. E. Moore (Ed.), *Cognitive Development and the Acquisition of Language* (pp. 111–144). New York: Academic Press.

Rosenbloom, R. S., McLaughlin, C. P., & Wolek, F. W. (1965). *Technology Transfer and the Flow of Technical Information in a Large Industrial Corporation*, 2 vols. Cambridge, MA: Graduate School of Business Administration, Harvard University.

Rosenbloom, R. S., & Wolek, F. W. (1966). Studies of the flow of technical information: An interim report. Graduate School of Business Administration, Harvard University, Cambridge, MA. January 1966.

Salton, G. (1968). *Automatic Information Organization and Retrieval.* New York: McGraw-Hill.

Salton, G., & Buckley, C. (1990). Improving retrieval performance by relevance feedback. *Journal of the American Society for Information Science,* 41, 288–297.

Saracevic, T. (2007). Relevance: A review of the literature and a framework for thinking on the notion in information science, Part II: Nature and manifestations of relevance. *Journal of the American Society for Information Science and Technology,* 58(3), 1915–1933.

Saxon, M. L., & Richardson, J. V. (2002). *Understanding Reference Transactions: Transforming an Art into a Science.* San Diego: Academic Press.

Schamber, L., Eisenberg, M. B., & Nilan, M. S. (1990). A re-examination of relevance: Toward a dynamic, situational definition. *Information Processing & Management,* 26(6), 755–776.

Shannon, C. E. (1949). The mathematical theory of communication. In C. E. Shannon & W. Weaver (Aus.), *The Mathematical Theory of Communication* (pp. 3–91). Urbana, IL: The University of Illinois Press.

Shen, X., Tan, B., & Zhai, C. (2005). Context-sensitive information retrieval using implicit feedback. In R. Baeza-Yates & N. Ziviani (Eds.), *Proceedings of the 28th Annual International ACM SIGIR Conference on Research and Development in Information Retrieval* (pp. 43–50). New York: ACM Press.

Smith, L. C. (1991). Memex as an image of potentiality revisited. In J. M. Nyce & P. Kahn (Eds.), *From Memex to Hypertext: Vannevar Bush and the Mind's Machine* (pp. 261–286). Boston: Academic Press.

Spink, A. (2010). *Information Behavior: An Evolutionary Instinct.* Berlin: Springer.

Spink, A., & Cole, C. (2006). Human Information Behavior: Integrating diverse approaches and information use. *Journal of the American Society for Information Science and Technology,* 57(1), 25–35.

Spink, A., & Cole, C. (2007). Information behavior: A socio-cognitive ability. *Evolutionary Psychology,* 5(2), 257–274. Accessed

September 30, 2011, from www.epjournal.net/filestore/EP05257 274.pdf.

Spink, A., Wilson, T. D., Ford, N. A., Foster, A., & Ellis, D. (2002a). Information seeking and mediated searching, Part I: Background and research design. *Journal of the American Society for Information Science and Technology*, 53(9), 695–703.

Spink, A., Wilson, T. D., Ford, N. A., Foster, A., & Ellis, D. (2002b). Information seeking and mediated searching, Part 3: Successive searching. *Journal of the American Society for Information Science and Technology*, 53(9), 716–727.

Svenonius, E. (2000). *The Intellectual Foundation of Information Organization*. Cambridge, MA: MIT Press.

Swanson, D. R. (1972). Requirements study for future catalogs. *Library Quarterly*, 42(3), 302–315.

Taylor, R. S. (1962). The process of asking questions. *American Documentation*, 13, 391–396.

Taylor, R. S. (1968). Question-negotiation and information seeking in libraries. *College & Research Libraries*, 29(3), 178–194.

Taylor, R. S. (1982). Value-added processes in the information life cycle. *Journal of the American Society for Information Science*, 33(5), 341–346.

Todd, R. J. (1999). Back to our beginnings: Information utilization, Bertram Brookes and the fundamental equation of information science. *Information Processing & Management*, 35, 851–870.

Urquhart, D. J. (1948). The distribution and use of scientific and technical information. *Journal of Documentation*, 3, 222–231.

University of California Libraries, Bibliographic Services Task Force (2005). Rethinking how we provide bibliographic services for the University of California. Accessed September 30, 2011, from libraries.universityofcalifornia.edu/sopag/BSTF/Final.pdf.

Vakkari, P. (2001). A theory of the task-based information retrieval process: A summary and generalization of a longitudinal study. *Journal of Documentation*, 57(1), 44–60.

Van der Veer Martens, B. (1999). Biographical note—Robert S. Taylor. *Journal of the American Society for Information Science*, 50(12), 1109–1110.

Wersig, G., & Windel, G. (1985). Information science needs a theory of "information actions." *Social Science Information Studies*, 5, 11–23.

Wildemuth, B. M., & O'Neill, A. L. (1995). The "known" in known-item searches: Empirical support for user-centered design. *College & Research Libraries*, 56(3), 265–281.

Wilson, T. D. (1981). On user studies and information needs. *Journal of Documentation*, 37(1), 3–15.

Wilson, T. D. (1999). Models in information behaviour research. *Journal of Documentation*, 55(3), 249–270.

Wilson, T. D. (2000). Human information behavior. *Informing Science*, 3(2), 49–55.

Wilson, T. D., Ford, N., Foster, D., Ellis, D., & Spink, A. (2002). Information seeking and mediated searching, Part 2: Uncertainty. *Journal of the American Society for Information Science and Technology*, 53(9), 704–715.

Wolek, F. W. (1970). The complexity of messages in science and engineering: An influence on patterns of communication. In C. E. Nelson and D. K. Pollock (Eds.), *Communication among Scientists and Engineers* (pp. 233–265). Lexington, MA: Heath Lexington Books.

Wynn, T., & Coolidge, F. L. (2004). The expert Neanderthal mind. *Journal of Human Evolution*, 46(4), 467–487.

About the Author

Charles Cole has been a researcher-writer in the information science field for nearly 20 years. Beginning with a 1990 lecture on information need given by T. D. Wilson, he became interested in the motivation and behavior of a person seeking information, particularly the information need that begins the process and controls the person's subsequent information search behavior. Under Wilson's and David Ellis's supervision at the University of Sheffield, Cole studied the information process of 45 history PhD students, with a focus on what triggered the process. Was it mostly inside the person—and thus a need—or was the information process triggered by something outside the person? Or is information need, as Wilson said, an innate cognitive tool or mechanism that humans utilize to satisfy the primary cognitive, affective, and physiological human needs?

In the last decade, Cole has expanded his interest in information need to designing information retrieval systems based on why and how humans naturally search for information when they are in a construction-of-focus phase of performing a task. Along with Jamshid Beheshti (PI) and Andrew Large, he is currently conducting a 3-year Canadian government (SSHRC)-funded study, which will ascertain and build information seeking fundamentals into a virtual environment for 12- to 13-year-old students researching a school assignment.

According to two recent bibliometric studies, Cole was the sixth-most prolific author of articles published in the *Journal of the American Society for Information Science and Technology* (JASIST) in the 2000–2007 period, and in a Web of Science study, was fourth in impact in the topic "evaluation [information retrieval]" in the decade 1991–2000. He has authored or co-authored over 40 articles in the top-ranked journals in information science, including *JASIST, Information Processing & Management, Library Quarterly,* and the *Annual Review of Information Science and Technology.* With Amanda Spink, he has edited two books in information science: *New Directions in Human Information Behavior* (2006) and *New Directions in Cognitive Information Retrieval* (2005), both recently published in paperback by Springer. He received his PhD (Information Science) in 1994 from the University of Sheffield, his

MLIS from McGill University in 1989, and his BA (History-Geography) from McGill University in 1978. He completed a 2-year postdoctoral fellowship at Concordia University in 1999. He is currently Researcher, Affiliated Member, at the School of Information Studies, McGill University. He is also a consultant (Colemining Inc.).

Index

Note: Page numbers followed by f and t indicate figures and tables, respectively.

Theories of Information Behavior

Edited by Karen E. Fisher, Sanda Erdelez, and Lynne (E. F.) McKechnie

This unique book presents authoritative overviews of more than 70 conceptual frameworks for understanding how people seek, manage, share, and use information in different contexts. Covering both established and newly proposed theories of information behavior, the book includes contributions from 85 scholars from 10 countries. Theory descriptions cover origins, propositions, methodological implications, usage, and links to related theories.

456 pp/hardbound/ISBN 978-1-57387-230-0
ASIST Members $39.60 • Nonmembers $49.50

Digital Inclusion

Measuring the Impact of Information and Community Technology

Edited by Michael Crandall and Karen E. Fisher

Through an examination of efforts by community technology organizations in Washington State, *Digital Inclusion* offers a model for educating policy makers about the actual impacts of such efforts, along with suggestions for practical implementation. The case studies and analyses presented here will be of critical interest to community technology centers, libraries, government service agencies, and any other organization (or funder) that uses technology to deliver services to the information poor.

200 pp/hardbound/ISBN 978-1-57387-373-4
ASIST Members $47.60 • Nonmembers $59.50

To order or for a complete catalog, contact:

Information Today, Inc.

143 Old Marlton Pike, Medford, NJ 08055 • 609/654-6266
email: custserv@infotoday.com • website: www.infotoday.com

More Titles of Interest from Information Today, Inc.

Introduction to Information Science and Technology

Edited by Charles H. Davis and Debora Shaw

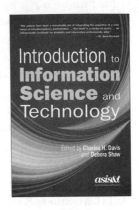

This guide to information science and technology presents a clear, concise, and approachable account of the fundamental issues, with appropriate historical background and theoretical background. Topics covered include information needs, seeking, and use; representation and organization of information; computers and networks; structured information systems; information systems applications; users' perspectives in information systems; social informatics; information policy; and the information profession.

288 pp/softbound/ISBN 978-1-57387-423-6
ASIST Members $47.60 • Nonmembers $59.50

Information Representation and Retrieval in the Digital Age, Second Edition

By Heting Chu

This second edition of Heting Chu's popular work on information representation and retrieval (IRR) features many updates and revisions, including coverage of taxonomies, folksonomies, ontologies, social tagging, and next generation OPACs. She reviews key concepts and major developmental stages of the field, and then examines information representation methods, IRR languages, retrieval techniques and models, and internet retrieval systems. In addition, she explains the retrieval of multilingual, multimedia, and hyper-structured information and explores the user dimension and evaluation issues.

320 pp/hardbound/ISBN 978-1-57387-393-2
ASIST Members $39.60 • Nonmembers $49.50